More Praise for *YOU! The Positive Force in Change*

"In this book, covering approaches ranging from neuroscience to emotional and social intelligence, Rogers and van Dam call our attention to the critical role each of us plays in developing the capabilities latent in everybody around us and in the organizations we live in. Offering practical advice and multiple examples they challenge us to create tomorrow today."
  -DR. SHLOMO BEN-HUR, Professor of Leadership and Organizational Behavior, IMD

"As Learning and Development professionals, Eileen and Nick's number one goal has always been to help others be successful, often in adverse, opportunistic and certainly ever changing circumstances. Their record performance is evidence of successful effectiveness. In this latest work, they combine their many years of practical experience with the latest research on neuroscience and positive psychology to provide practical and insightful advice for individuals and organizations. If you are looking for ways to drive change and extraordinary performance, then this book is for YOU!"
  -JAMES WALL, Retired Chief Talent and Diversity Officer, Deloitte Touche Tohmatsu Limited

"YOU! is a must read for leaders grappling with change and complexity. A wonderful, rich resource sharing the latest findings in neuroscience and guidelines on how to build a resilient, optimistic and engaged organizational culture."
  -AMY ELIZABETH FOX, CEO, Mobius Executive Leadership

"Change in life is a given, getting up and moving forward is a choice! Can you re-contract yourself and build the confidence to face new challenges? I'm sure most of you can flourish and discover new territory. YOU! is just a terrific resource for personal growth!"
  -JAN RIJKEN, Global Head of Learning & Talent at KPMG

"Nick and Eileen's experience and wisdom is unparalleled and this book is yet another classic. People in pursuit of enhancing their effectiveness and wishing to keep learning will find this very useful. A must read for people who are intellectually curious!"
  -YASH MAHADIK, SVP/Head of HR Business Transformation, IT & Global Head of Learning, Philips

About this Book

Change is hard! For individuals and organizations. But the twenty-first century demand for frequent, successful, transformational change is rising exponentially. Recent dynamic findings of neuroscience and positive psychology provide surprising insights into why the brain is not inclined to change and how to lead successful positive change that engages both the mind and the heart.

In their valuable book, Eileen and Nick share vital brain-based approaches to leading positive change – illustrated by real-world examples. By presenting the hard science in terms that are useful to the non-scientist, practical applications of brain function show how to achieve meaningful and sustainable change.

You can apply these methods to change your own mind-set and increase your ability to be flexible, adaptive, creative, and innovative. Also, you can leverage these tools to set the vision, meaning, motivation, pace and tone for teams and organizations to achieve extraordinary results.

YOU!

THE POSITIVE FORCE IN CHANGE

Leveraging Insights
from Neuroscience and
Positive Psychology

EILEEN ROGERS & NICK VAN DAM

ISBN: 978-1-4834-1814-8 (sc)
ISBN: 978-1-4834-1815-5 (hc)
ISBN: 978-1-4834-1813-1 (e)

Library of Congress Control Number: 2014918150

Published by Lulu, last revised 12/8/2014

Dedication

We are grateful to all the people in our lives who have supported and contributed to our positivity, optimism, and joy and most of all for the love shared.

Contents

Foreword

Like many others, Eileen and Nick have enjoyed lives embracing both positive experiences and the affirmative growth that can be gained by learning from adversity. Since Eileen and Nick first met and over the subsequent years, they found that they share a deep interest and appreciation for the growing discoveries in the fields of cognitive neuroscience and positive psychology. Their enthusiasm for the research, and its application by leaders, teams and enterprises to address the challenges of the twenty-first century, is the inspiration for writing this book.

Eileen and Nick have the same number one Strength on the Gallup StrengthsFinder® assessment, *Ideation* – the pleasure and near perfect performance of generating creative and innovative ideas. This shared Strength drove a constant and dynamic exchange between them as they uncovered new insights coming out of this vibrant and growing discipline.

As professionals in learning and development, their focus has always been on providing opportunities for others to master key competencies and capabilities, empowering the achievement of ever higher performance and increased enjoyment and satisfaction in lives and at work. The research discoveries, concepts, and mind-sets from this revolutionary field offer tremendous advancements for individuals and groups of people to pursue very different styles of leadership adaptive to the demands of the twenty-first century and to create cultures of engagement, commitment, and growth. Eileen and Nick now actively apply these concepts and practices in their consulting engagements and leadership programs in order to support the development of positive lives, relationships and organizations.

In this book, it is their goal to offer a high-level understanding of the concepts of cognitive neuroscience and positive psychology, while also providing a better understanding of a variety of sub-fields related to the scientific research on how the brain really works. What is described should have a significant impact on how we organize, manage, motivate, and reward performance in the twenty-first century.

There is of course much to choose from in preparing a book like this. We have tried to include some of the most important findings and theories that are coming out of the robust research. The framework below depicts what we have chosen to include:

Cognitive Neuroscience & Positive Psychology		
PERSONAL POSITIVITY	POSITIVE RELATIONSHIPS	POSITIVE ORGANIZATIONS
• Leveraging Strengths	• Building Trust	• Employing Appreciative Inquiry
• Practicing Mindfulness	• Generating Emotional & Social Intelligence	• Coaching for Positive Change
• Pursuing Optimism & Positivity		• Fostering Engagement & Flow
• Discovering Happiness		

Since rapid change is impacting all of us, we urgently need new approaches to master the moment. The contents of this book should appeal to all who want to transform the quality of their lives and work. Leaders and individuals in all fields of endeavor – whether business, government, NGOs, religion, education, medicine, psychology or simply families – should find the research-based tools, techniques, and methods useful and be able to apply these immediately.

Cognitive neuroscience and positive psychology provide the building blocks to transform the incessant and disruptive change demanded by the twenty-first century from being a source of fear, demotivation, and resistance, to becoming a clear roadmap for growth and development. The field continues to advance, ever more rapidly in recent years. Therefore, we intend to keep our focus as the future evolves and will continue to provide information and insights into the surprising innovations arising out of this research to our colleagues.

YOU! The Positive Force in Change

Purpose and Outcomes

This chapter introduces the themes of the book – the neuroscience of leading positive change, and the practices to lead change in a world that relentlessly demands flexibility, adaptability, resilience, and meaning.

Everyone has moments of leadership, no matter the role or the title in the organization. These are the times when we add value and meaning, ask probing questions, challenge the status quo, provide the focus that inspires others, and engage in peak performance. These are the leadership moments.

The question always arises: *"Are leaders born or made?"* In response, Jim Kouzes, leadership guru and author, says, *"I've never met a leader who was not born!"* In fact, we all have the potential to be leaders and the mandate to develop and build leaders has never been more urgent.

> **Most people today fall outrageously short of their potential. A goal of the twenty-first century should be to develop the capability latent in everybody by expanding human potential.**
> ∞ James Martin, author and founder of the 21st Century Institute, Oxford University

As we face the unbelievable complexity of our century, our existing mental models limit and filter what we see and understand and ultimately our performance. Traditional science and neoclassical management have typically focused on only one problem at a time. But the game has changed. The old solutions are not working any more. It is not enough to spend time solving past problems with outdated solutions. If you try to patch the old system, it becomes unmanageable.

One problem cannot be solved without considering the interdependent variables. Because as soon as there is a change in one, it immediately begins to impact and change the others. Sometimes called the *butterfly effect,* chaos theory finds that a small change at one place in a complex system can have large impacts elsewhere. Much as a butterfly flapping its wings in Thailand might contribute to the development of a hurricane in the Atlantic. In business this systems dynamic has been seen in the organizations that use *Kaizen,* which in Japanese means *good change.* This process achieves daily small improvements (the butterfly) throughout the entire organization, at every level. By monitoring the results, adjusting and adopting the improvement, organizational alignment around the change is fostered.

Using a similar Kaizen approach, we must identify and define the new problems of our century first, since 60 percent of the solution is an accurate definition of the problem. To do this we need to begin with a clean sheet and create new mental maps. Given the evidence, a whole systems approach to driving positive change in our organizations is required to create and sustain productivity, innovation, profits, and engagement. And the research-based practices that enable us to build these new organizations have come to hand!

At the same time that the chaos, complexity, and choice in the twenty-first century are increasing, the fields of neuroscience, technology, psychology, medicine, sociology, education and management are merging to uncover what drives successful change in humans and in organizations. Increasingly, the focus has coalesced around the incredible impact that happiness and positivity have in fostering the vibrant capacity to adapt, flex, and embrace change. The research shows that the former belief that happiness is the outcome of success is in fact wrong.

> *Thanks to cutting-edge science, we now know that happiness is the precursor of success...happiness and optimism actually fuel performance and achievement.*
> ∞Shawn Achor, educator, author, and speaker

As you explore the chapters of this book, think about the application potential to your own life and your work. As you embrace and drive personal changes, you will create a positive environment around you that resonates with others. Our emotions and the small, continuous improvements in our behavior are contagious and have a potential ripple effect to the third degree of relatedness, estimated to be approximately 1,000 people in each person's social network. Stand straight and smile, already this change drives your brain to send out neurochemicals that actually make you happy! And you will make others happy too!

So you can use the techniques described in each chapter on both a personal and an organizational basis. And each chapter has examples of companies that are embracing these changes to prepare for future success.

Chapter 1: The Neuroscience of Leading Positive Change – the discoveries of brain research compel a total overhaul of our current human systems, organizational structures, performance management, motivation, and reward systems.

Chapter 2: Pursuing Optimism and Positivity – the importance of optimism and positivity to a life that is successful and satisfying have been proven by research and there are methods to build this capability.

Chapter 3: Practicing Mindfulness – uncluttering the brain by using a mindfulness routine, clarifies thinking, focuses the mind, reduces the confusion of stress and opens the brain to possibilities and opportunities.

Chapter 4: Generating Emotional and Social Intelligence – the exercise of emotional intelligence has been traced in the brain and can be built to foster empathy and rapport with others.

Chapter 5: Leveraging Strengths – inner talent, values, and strengths founded on these talents are well-traveled deep neural pathways that can be measured and provide an enduring source of well-being.

Chapter 6: Fostering Engagement and Flow – the contributions of full engagement at work to productivity and profitability are undeniable and a life in *flow* should be the goal of every individual and organization.

Chapter 7: Building Trust – trust is the foundation of great relationships, teams and organizations, without which no success is possible. Building and sustaining trust is an imperative today.

Chapter 8: Employing Appreciative Inquiry – this process for driving positive change focuses people's minds on a positive future state built on the good that already exists, making it feasible, achievable, and removing the distrust and inherent fear of change.

Chapter 9: Coaching for Positive Change – the world of information and knowledge changes completely how we manage people's performance. No longer following the linear tasks of the past, the workers of today must solve complex problems that require peak performance, and this is best brought about through a positive coaching relationship.

Chapter 10: The Future Now – A quick touch on the concepts of happiness and flourishing and the next steps in pursuing the creation of positive organizations, teams, and improving people's lives, based on the discoveries of neuroscience.

Enjoy!

CHAPTER 1

The Neuroscience of Leading Positive Change

Purpose and Outcomes

This chapter explores the collaboration and recent discoveries among psychology, neuroscience, medicine, education, and management to describe ways in which evidence-based brain science can be leveraged to lead positive change.

This chapter reveals:
- that the brain is not static in adulthood, but capable of growth and change throughout a lifetime
- the steps to changing habits of the brain and consequent behaviors
- the role that *attention density* plays in building strong positive neural pathways, and how this phenomenon can be used to foster and embed change in behaviors
- the impact of social networks and interactions on building higher productivity, engagement, empathy, and rapport

---

If we want to lead successful positive change, what must we do? Brain research again finds that the best leaders begin with themselves! When we transform ourselves, we can support others to begin their own journey on the path to a positive, flexible, and adaptive view of change. Building a whole new brain, focused on positive strengths, equips leaders to be highly successful at work, in life and in driving positive change in the twenty-first century.

In this sense, there is much to be learned from an unknown monk, whose CE 1100 tomb in England provides a profound insight that is highly relevant to us today.

> *When I was a young man, I wanted to change the world.*
> *I found it was difficult to change the world, so I tried to change my nation.*
>
> *When I found I couldn't change the nation, I began to focus on my town.*
> *I couldn't change the town, and as an older man, I tried to change my family.*
>
> *Now, as an old man, I realize the only thing I can change is myself, and suddenly I realize that if long ago I had changed myself, I could have made an impact on my family.*
>
> *My family and I could have made an impact on our town. Their impact could have changed the nation and I could indeed have changed the world.*

What is the Neuroscience of Brain Research?

Neuroscience is the study of the entire nervous system in the body. The emerging field of brain research draws upon several aspects of neuroscience to unlock the mysteries of how the brain really works. The discoveries over the past three decades have revealed that current practices in organizing, managing and rewarding performance are wrong, and in fact are practically designed to demotivate peak performance. On the other hand, these findings allow us to discover and apply new ways to leverage the brain's inherent function and capacities to achieve higher performance and results.

Concepts of neuroscience have created a deeper understanding of **how and why** a positive focus on strengths, optimism, engagement, emotional intelligence, relationships, appreciative inquiry and mindfulness contribute to a meaningful and satisfying life.

Some companies are already recognizing these astounding, scientifically proven discoveries in brain science, and they are actively integrating new practices into their organizations based on how the brain actually operates.

Apple Inc.: One example is Apple's *Think Different* campaign, with ads that stated:

- *To the crazy ones.*
- *Here's to the misfits. The rebels. The troublemakers.*
- *Here's to the ones who see the world differently.*
- *They're the ones who invent and imagine and create.*

- *They're the ones who push the human race forward.*
- *While some may see them as the crazy ones, we see genius.*
- *Because the people who are crazy enough to believe they can change the world are the ones who actually do.*

Fade to Apple logo and line "Think different."

Google: Another example is Google's practice of having employees work 20 percent of their time on whatever interests them, appealing to the human inherent desire for autonomy, mastery and purpose to ignite motivation.[1] Of course, Google owns the intellectual property rights of what is produced during that time, and the benefits are prodigious. More than half of the innovations that Google introduces each year are created during this 20 percent time.

Facebook: Finally, there is another example of the application of positive psychology being implemented in a very successful company. Facebook is integrating the practice of leveraging strengths to support engagement and peak performance.

> **At Facebook, we try to be a strengths-based organization...we focus on people's natural strengths and spend our management time trying to find ways for them to use those strengths every day.**
> ∞Sheryl Sandberg, Chief Operating Officer, Facebook

However, these discoveries are not yet widely understood and for the most part not practiced by most organizations, which first must **unlearn** the twentieth century methods of:

- hierarchy
- control
- static position descriptions
- focus on problems that need to be solved rather than opportunities waiting to be realized
- *carrot/stick* performance rewards
- obsession with producing shareholder value rather than achieving a meaningful purpose

---

[1] Daniel H. Pink, *Drive: The Surprising Truth About What Motivates Us,* Canongate Books Ltd., 2009, p.96.

And so much more that is actually based more on myth than science. These former (and unfortunately still current) organizational practices are found to be fully outdated due to the daily contributions of discoveries in brain research!

> *Education is what is left after you've forgotten everything you've learned.*
>
> ∞Albert Einstein, theoretical physicist

On the other hand, examples of companies achieving amazing success by adopting new practices based on brain science findings are found throughout this book.

The Brain can Grow and Change During a Lifetime

In the past century, modern science held the belief that human potential is fixed and that the mature brain is static after adolescence. In the past three decades, neuroscience has combined in powerful ways with chemistry, technology, and medicine along with other disciplines such as psychology and education, to contribute major advances in brain research. Using fMRI and PET[2] scans combined with the measurements of neurotransmitters – the chemicals that allow neurons in the brain to communicate with each other – researchers can observe what is actually happening in the brain as it undertakes different tasks and experiences varied emotions. One amazing discovery is that the brain is **not** static – completely developed and unchangeable after adulthood – but elastic and capable of change even in old age. This is called *neuroplasticity.*

There is empirical proof that the brain is flexible and can transform with intention, attention, and deliberate practice. Multiple research results have mapped increased growth of grey matter in the brain, when a focused effort is made to pay attention to something in a particular way. Rather than a *fixed* brain, using a mind-set of a *growth* brain supports creativity, innovation, and positive emotions.

---

[2] fMRI (Functional Magnetic Resonance Imaging) PET (Positron Emission Tomography).

Thinking About Thinking

Humans are the only living creatures that can actively think about thinking. This is called *metacognition* – the ability to recognize and think about the processes used to plan, monitor, and assess one's understanding and performance. Frequently traveled neural pathways embed deeply in the brain and become unconscious routines that are quickly traveled – habits of thought, values, and behavior. Abraham Maslow depicts this process very well in his stages of learning.

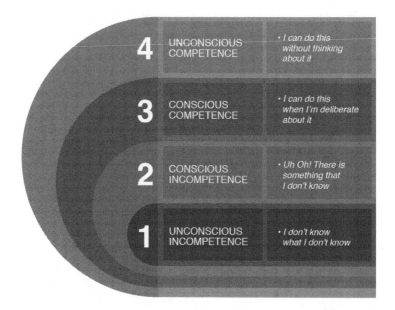

Metacognition brings information and knowledge from the unconscious into the conscious mind where it is shaped and then restored into the unconscious mind. During this process we can challenge ourselves at the core of our being. By recognizing our own habitual neural pathways, we can make a **choice** to practice positive thinking often enough that the patterns embedded in the brain become our *unconscious competence* and support our positive perceptions.

Changing Your Mind-set

Thus, humans can actually use their mind to change their brain for the better. Leveraging metacognition, we have a choice to either follow negative rumination and painful thoughts, shutting down potential and growth, or to intentionally pursue a cognitive pattern that seeks the positive and keeps the brain open to possibilities and opportunities. Shutting off negative or painful thoughts actually decreases the sense of pain, while focusing on the positive lowers activation of the amygdala. (See Chapter 4, pages 50–51)

This brings us to the practices of successful change leaders. Growth minded leaders begin with a strong belief in human potential, their own and that of others, to change for the better. In the twenty-first century this is greatly needed, because brain research has demonstrated that change is a significant challenge for the brain. The brain has a tendency toward *stasis* – a state of inactivity or equilibrium – and a negativity bias. This is why breaking old habits and embedded thought patterns are so difficult. The impact of a negative experience goes far deeper and lasts longer than a positive one. Making it imperative to focus on and build positive neural pathways to overcome both the negativity bias and stasis.

Because a plan is not a decision to act, one way to overcome this is to progress toward a change goal with small steps. With each decision to take a small progressive step, there is a gradual related increase in the brain's commitment to it. Once we have decided to do something, the brain develops an emotional commitment to it. This focus is called *attention density*. In his groundbreaking book, Charles Duhigg emphasizes that this only happens when the brain's assessment is that the action will offer more benefit than the perceived losses. The reward center of the brain informs the action centers that the action is needed **and** is beneficial.[3] Without this process, the brain reacts with resistance to change.

The fact that our thoughts create our lives has been recognized throughout the centuries, even without modern technology!

> *Our life is what our thoughts make of it.*
> ∞Marcus Aurelius, CE 121 – 180, Roman Emperor

---

[3] Charles Duhigg, *The Power of Habit; Why we do what we do and how to change*, Random House, 2013.

Neuroscience as a Positive Force in Change

The twenty-first century presents us with a world of complexity, chaos, diversity, challenge and change. Change today is both persistent and pervasive, and...unstoppable. The navigation of such difficult and unknown terrain demands new mental models in individuals, teams and organizations – the mastery of a whole new mind-set.

Fortunately, the fields of psychology, neuroscience, medicine, management and education are actively seeking answers to uncover how we can do this. What is being discovered turns current organizational practices upside down.

Optimism and Positivity

Brain research supports the importance of a shared compelling vision of an ideal, possible future state, because it motivates present behavior toward the future desired goal. In the brain, a guiding principle or image focuses attention on the hypothetical positive outcome. By using visuals, data and images, and navigating with small steps toward the goal, it is possible to inspire emotional commitment to the desired future – moving away from uninspiring *corporate speak* to appeal to the multiple intelligences identified by Howard Gardner.[4]

Focusing on calamities, misfortunes and heartbreaks causes the brain to create more pain. Eventually, this rut of negativity leads to cognitive distortions and catastrophizing events. Even though your brain's natural tendency is to be negative, using the positive explanatory style of optimists actually refocuses the brain. (See Chapter 2, page 23) And optimism combined with hope (the sense that a realistic, eventual solution is possible) keeps opportunity alive and is shown to displace fear from the amygdala.

Mindfulness

Practicing mindfulness clears the brain of external and internal *noise* and a calm mind is the key to thinking clearly. Inner strengths are built from inside the brain. Feeling and taking in positive experiences in simple, every day moments empowers positive experience of the present moment. Rick Hanson recommends building the brain's positive focus by practicing the

---

[4] Howard Gardner, *Frames of Mind: The Theory of Multiple Intelligences*, Basic Books, 2011.

mindful habit of **savoring** it, so it becomes enriched and embedded in the brain. *"The greater the duration, intensity, multimodality, novelty and personal relevance, the greater retention in the memory"*.[5]

Hanson suggests when we experience something good, we pay focused attention to it, expand and sustain it for some time in consciousness, magnify its intensity by involving all of the senses in the whole body, and look for unexpected rewards that result from the good experience. The natural propensity of the brain to magnify dangers and ignore positive experiences can be overcome. And, in turn, this changes your brain and ultimately your life!

> *Touching the ultimate dimension, we feel happy and comfortable, like the birds enjoying the blue sky or the deer enjoying the green fields. We know that we do not have to look for the ultimate outside of ourselves– it is available within us, in this very moment.*
>
> ∞Thich Nhat Hanh, Zen teacher

When the brain focuses on good news and positive experiences, the mind releases dopamine (a neurotransmitter which plays a major role in reward-motivated behavior). This causes the amygdala to react more intensely to the good, making the brain more aligned to attend, absorb and retain positive thoughts and feelings. Because the brain is a complex system of fast and complex feedback loops – 100 billion neurons with half a quadrillion connections – this practice builds a positive neural structure, a virtuous circle in the feedback loop.

The principle in neuroscience that *"Neurons that fire together, wire together"* is highly active in this practice. Positive mental states become positive neural traits!

Emotional and Social Intelligence

The body actually has three sources of intelligence! In the head, the heart and the gut.[6]

---

[5] Rick Hanson, *Hardwiring Happiness: The New Brain Science of Contentment, Calm and Confidence*, Harmony Books, 2013, p.111.
[6] Robert K. Cooper, *The Other 90%: How to Unlock Your Vast Untapped Potential for Leadership and Life*, Three Rivers Press, 2001, pp. 12 – 25.

All of these sources of insight, experience, and knowledge, are in constant communication – an integrated symphony of neurons, neurotransmitters and enzymes. These combine to create the source of *intuition* – the amazing capability in humans to recognize patterns before they arise to the conscious brain. It is a potent combination of our emotional and intellectual capabilities combined with our experiences that give rise to intuition...the *gut feeling*... and when we ignore it, we ignore it at our own peril!

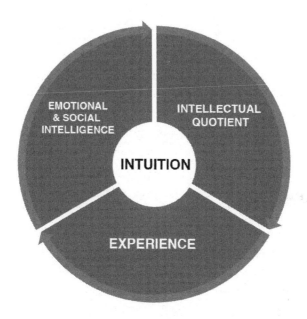

The amygdala alarm system and the unrelenting feelings of stress described in Chapter 4, on pages 48–49, send out demands for adrenalin, cortisol and norepinephrine, all of which are designed to protect us from acute catastrophe – such as a charging lion or when we are engaged in warfare – and these neurotransmitters pull blood flow into the core of the body, increasing muscle tension and heart rate. At the same time, they decrease flow to vital functions, such as digestion, cohesive heart rhythms, reproductive drive, and immunity.

When these hormones go unregulated due to stress in our modern environment, they increase reactivity to the negative. Negative rumination creates chronic elevated levels of cortisol, called the stress hormone, creating a compounded negative physical impact.

Trust Relationships

Our brains are constantly interacting with the brains of others – in the family, on teams, in society, and in organizations with positive or negative outcomes. Several studies have shown that positive social relationships have the most impact on overall happiness, success, heightened well-being, and lowered stress throughout life.

One of these studies, called the Harvard Men study, a longitudinal psychological study of 268 Harvard graduates that has run for 78 years, has allowed scientists to determine what life characteristics and personal qualities have led to the happiest, most satisfying lives as opposed to those with the least positive outcomes. George Valliant, who led the study for several decades, was asked by Atlantic Monthly, what had he learned from the study, he said *"That the only thing that really matters in life are your relationships to other people. What matters is love, full stop."*[7]

Richard Boyatsis, who has written extensively on the neuroscience discoveries that can produce a positive impact on leadership practices, finds that there is a broad difference in the practice of social intelligence by *resonant* (high quality relationship) leaders versus those he terms *dissonant* (low quality relationship) leaders.[8] He joined with other researchers to observe the brain activity of middle-aged individuals when they were asked to recall experiences with resonant leaders versus dissonant leaders. The results were highly revealing as to what occurs when the brain contemplates experiences with resonant leaders – 14 regions of interest were activated in the brain, including the attention, social network, mirror system, and other regions associated with approach relationships. Whereas, the brain activity of those recalling encounters with dissonant leaders activated only 6 regions of interest and deactivated 11!

The implications are that dissonant leaders actually *turn people off*, whereas those who build resonant relationships activate openness to new ideas and a more social orientation to others.[9] The proposition here is that leaders should first put emphasis on social intelligence and relationships, and next on obtaining results...the outcomes will be greatly improved.

---

[7] Joshua Wolf Shank, 'What Makes us Happy?', *Atlantic Monthly*, June 2009, p.3.

[8] Richard Boyatzis, *Neuroscience and Leadership: The Promise of Insights*, Ivey Business Journal, January/February 2011.

[9] Richard Boyatsis, Annie McKee, *Resonant Leadership: Renewing Yourself and Connecting with Others Through Mindfulness, Hope, and Compassion*, Harvard Business School Publishing, 2005.

Strengths

In Chapter 5, the process of building talents, mental capacities, and values into strengths, is described as the embedding of frequently traveled neural pathways into long-term memory. The building of *unconscious competence* enables you to perform work related to that strength with ease, joy, and near perfect performance every time. The neural pattern that supports this development was also described earlier in this chapter.

Most importantly, in order to achieve peak performance and find life and work satisfaction, being able to use your personal strengths is one of the most enduring sources of well-being. Loving what you do relies upon linking your sense of purpose and passion with work – empowering you to contribute at your highest potential.[10] Using unhindered strengths, children experience a constant flow of *autotelic* experiences – an activity that has purpose contained within and part of itself. In work, if the highest strengths and talents are leveraged, an autotelic mind-set of possibility, joy, and dedication arises, and this produces engagement and flow along with extraordinary results.

Engagement and Flow

Brain imaging has found that visualizing or imagining an action stimulates the same region of the brain as the actual performance of the action.[11]
∞Srinivisan S. Pillay, Professor of Psychiatry,
Harvard Medical School Faculty

Many of us have had the experience of being on a skiing vacation and spending the evenings enjoying videos of great skiers as they take on the steep, unspoiled slopes of amazing mountains. We sense every move of the expert skier in our own bodies. It turns out that in the anticipation of an event, the brain acts on our prediction of what will happen next. So if we set our brain on anticipation of peak performance on the slopes, the brain fires in harmony with that image of success as if it were actually happening. This fact is highly relevant to our efforts to motivate performance.

---

[10] David DiSalvo, *Brain Changer: How Harnessing Your Brain's Power to Adapt Can Change Your Life*, BenBella Books, Inc. 2013, p. 122.
[11] Srinivisan S. Pillay, *Your Brain and Business*, FT Press, 2011, p. 144.

Much work has been done on what truly motivates people. Research is finding that our current *motivational practices* in families, on teams and in organizations, in fact destroy intrinsic motivation and creativity, produce poor results, foster short-term thinking and defeat good behavior.[12] In his amazing book, Daniel Pink states at the opening: *"In the first ten years of this century – a period of truly staggering underachievement in business, technology and social progress – we've discovered that the sturdy, old operating system...is proving incompatible with many aspects of contemporary business."*

Pink cites many reasons for this, including the changing nature of work and economies, the new social goals of the millennial generation, and a desire for the experiences of engagement and flow. The solutions proposed in his book for creating flexible, adaptive organizations are firmly rooted in brain research findings.

The research shows that the brain has a *reward center* that lights up differently when people are offered diverse types of rewards. The work of Edward Deci, has found that the *if/then* reward system currently in force in our organizations, and that we strongly believe would motivate people – *If you do this...Then you will receive a reward* – is dead wrong. Although extrinsic rewards worked in the routine type of work dominant in the industrial age, which required linear thinking and the application of pre-set solutions to achieve success, Deci finds that brain research has demonstrated that this *so called* reward system is absolutely demotivating and destroys creativity and innovation.

> **When money is used as an external reward for some activity,
> the subjects lose intrinsic interest for the activity.**[13]
> ∞Edward Deci, Professor of Psychology and Gowen Professor
> in the Social Sciences, University of Rochester

The *heuristic* thinking (thinking that focuses on learning, discovery, or problem-solving by experimental and especially trial-and-error methods)[14] required to meet the challenges of creativity, flexibility, innovative problem

---

[12] Daniel H. Pink, *Drive: The Surprising Truth About What Motivates Us*, Canongate Books Ltd., 2009, p.59.

[13] Edward I. Deci, 'The Effects of Externally Mediated Rewards on Intrinsic Motivation', *Journal of Personality and Social Psychology*, 18, 1971, pp. 119 - 120.

[14] Miriam-Webster Online Dictionary.

solving in the twenty-first century is quite different from the if-then model. In 2000, Ryan and Deci conducted an exhaustive study on reward usage in 128 experiments. Their comparisons of these findings led to the firm conclusion that the use of the if/then *extrinsic* rewards have a primarily negative impact on people's greatest source of motivation, which is *intrinsic* – the desire to do something because it is interesting, challenging, and inherently enjoyable.[15] And it is intrinsic motivation that drives the heuristic thinking so needed today.

Daniel Pink builds on Deci's discovery in his work by providing a formula with three components. These rely not on if/then rewards, but on rewards that are based on *now...that* completion of more complex, conceptual problems. The three components are mastery, autonomy and purpose[16]:

MASTERY

• Intense practice to master something
• Small measures of improvement over time
• Setbacks seen as learning to guide the future

AUTONOMY

Control over choices of:
• What task to commit to
• When to do the work
• How to do it
• With whom to work

PURPOSE

• Knowing and believing in the meaning of work
• Boundaries between work and play non-existant
• Doing something beyond the self

---

[15] Richard M. Ryan and Edward I. Deci, 'Extrinsic and Intrinsic Motivations: Classic Definitions and New Directions', *Contemporary Educational Psychology*, 2000, v. 25, pp. 54 – 67.
[16] Daniel H. Pink, *Drive: The Surprising Truth About What Motivates Us*, Canongate Books Ltd., 2009.

With a focus on purpose, alternative business models have also emerged that challenge the predominant shareholder model. These new business models are termed *not just for profit* organizations. These companies pursue a dual intention: profits **and** purpose. In this very different approach, the drivers are to make enough profit to be self-sustaining while simultaneously serving a meaningful purpose.

> *Efficiency is doing things right: effectiveness is doing the right things.*
>
> ∞Peter Drucker, Claremont Graduate School
> professor and management guru

Companies such as **Grameen Danone Foods, Ltd** (www.danonecommunities.com) and **Toms Shoes** exemplify this new model where ethical capitalism, social entrepreneurship and other positive trends are leveraged to create a for-profit company with giving to society at its core. The positive core purpose of Grameen Danone is to provide excellent nutrition for low income, nutritionally deprived populations in Bangladesh, and Toms Shoes declares their positive core purpose on their website:

> *With every product you purchase, TOMS will help a person in need. One for One.®*
>
> ∞www.toms.com

Appreciative Inquiry

In order to think and decide effectively on course of action, the brain simultaneously and sequentially draws upon multiple centers – the emotional center, the risk center, the reward center and other regions – sending this information to the frontal cortex, the *executive function* of the brain. This drives whole brain thinking and more intelligent and successful outcomes.

Similarly Appreciative Inquiry (AI) draws upon the collective *organizational brain* to gather multiple perspectives that inform the organization's frontal cortex – or the executive committee – where then the best choices are fully informed in a holistic, comprehensive manner. The focus is on the positive and the ideal future. This *whole brain thinking* organizational process recognizes that we live in a world of interdependencies that demand both sustainability and viability, while rejecting a short-term performance focus. This perspective also requires a new style of leadership, one capable of integrating the interactions of dynamic systems in a multi-minded environment. The **AI** process supports both.

AI focuses on the growth mind-set eloquently described by Carol Dweck. Based on extensive research, Dweck notes that there is a vast difference between a *fixed mind-set* and a *growth mind-set* and she describes the impact each has on how we view challenges, obstacles, effort, criticism, and the success of others.

> *Mind-sets change what people strive for and what they see as success...they change the definition, significance and impact of failure...they change the deepest meaning of effort.*[17]
> ∞Carol Dweck, Lewis and Virginia Eaton Professor
> of Psychology, Stanford University

According to the research and brain science, the fixed mind-set avoids negative feedback and clings to what is known and what has produced success and recognition in the past. This mind-set acts on measurement against a pre-set standard of success and a morbid fear of failure. The growth mind-set sees performance through a very different lens, seeks and thrives on challenge and regards failure as a learning experience to fuel a new level of performance. Our mind-set, both conscious and unconscious, has a profound impact on what we can actually achieve.

The focus on the positive core of the enterprise in the **AI** methodology is supported by the brain science already described in this chapter. By concentrating attention on *"What is going right around here?"* and *"How can we leverage this to identify and achieve new opportunities?"*, the grey matter of the individual and collective brain in the enterprise are encouraged to grow in positive and productive ways. **AI** rewires the brain of the enterprise from a fixed mind-set to a growth mind-set.

Imagining the ideal future, drives out negative thinking and motivates behavior in the present towards the goal by focusing attention density on a positive outcome rather than fear of change.

---

[17] Carol Dweck, *Mindset the New Psychology of Success*, Ballantine Books, 2008, p. 46.

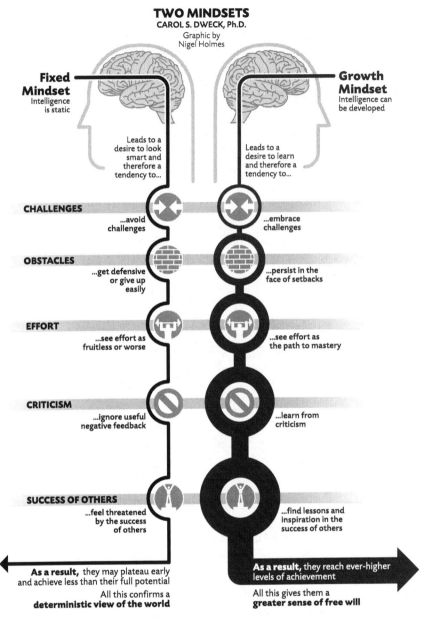

TWO MINDSETS
CAROL S. DWECK, Ph.D.
Graphic by
Nigel Holmes

Fixed Mindset
Intelligence is static

Growth Mindset
Intelligence can be developed

Leads to a desire to look smart and therefore a tendency to...

Leads to a desire to learn and therefore a tendency to...

CHALLENGES
...avoid challenges

...embrace challenges

OBSTACLES
...get defensive or give up easily

...persist in the face of setbacks

EFFORT
...see effort as fruitless or worse

...see effort as the path to mastery

CRITICISM
...ignore useful negative feedback

...learn from criticism

SUCCESS OF OTHERS
...feel threatened by the success of others

...find lessons and inspiration in the success of others

As a result, they may plateau early and achieve less than their full potential

As a result, they reach ever-higher levels of achievement

All this confirms a **deterministic view of the world**

All this gives them a **greater sense of free will**

Reprinted with permission

Coaching Mind-set

All that we have learned from brain research on organizing, motivating and managing performance indicates that our current approach, processes, and methods are wrong. As mentioned, these systems are more based on the military model deriving from the nineteenth and twentieth centuries of hierarchy, linear thinking, carrot/stick reward systems, problem identification and solving, static, prescribed positions, and fear of failure. And yet, for many reasons, this century demands innovative, creative, out-of-the-box thinking, and recognition and realization of new opportunities. Many enterprises are seeking this dynamic capability from their workers, but are still maintaining the old human systems, in a self-defeating, self-perpetuating vicious cycle.

A change can be driven in part by a new style of leadership in the organization – a resonant style – that supports full engagement. One key skill for these leaders is the art of questioning and listening, captured in a coaching approach to motivating high performance. The role of the coach is intrinsic to the role of managers and leaders as it fosters the basis of a strong relationship, deepened trust and a growth mind-set.

> *The ability to create a context for change – is what coaching,*
> *management and leadership are all about.*
> ∞Srinivasan S. Pillay, Professor of Psychiatry, Harvard Medical School

The brain research conducted by Pillay among others applies key findings in neuroscience discoveries to the process of coaching in powerful ways.[18]

PSYCHOLOGICAL MODEL	NEUROSCIENCE	COACHING APPLICATION
COMMITMENT IS NECESSARY TO DRIVE ACTION	Action orientation only arises when the left frontal cortex is engaged	Distinguish between plans and action orientation
VISUALIZATION HELPS YOU TO ACHIEVE YOUR GOAL	Imagery activates the action center of the brain	Ask questions that encourage visualization of the action
HOW YOU SPEAK AFFECTS HOW YOU ACT	Verbs stimulate the action centers of the brain	Encourage the use of verbs and action-oriented language
INNER CALM IS NECESSARY TO CLEAR THINKING	Silencing inner chaos affects short-term memory and attention	Work to identify the inner chaos that is leading to being 'stuck'
FOCUS INCREASES PRODUCTIVITY AND ABILITY TO CHANGE	Sort-term memory exercises that focus attention help bring the brain to action	Support movement from past/long-term memory to activate the needed energy in the frontal cortex
DEPRESSION IS DEMOTIVATING	Depression closes down the action centers in the brain	Assist in reframe of depressing situations

---

[18] Srinivasan S. Pillay, *Your Brain and Business: The Neuroscience of Great Leaders*, FT Press 2011, pp. 150 - 151.

Performance is largely founded on long-term memory, demonstrated above in the attainment of unconscious competence. And yet, when these neural pathways must change to accomplish new tasks, how can the old pathways be overcome? Using a combination of neuroscience and behavioral observations, Charles Duhigg has made an enormously important contribution to understanding how habits are formed and how they can be changed, which he published in his book, *The Power of Habit: Why we do what we do and how to change.*[19]

Recognizing that old habits actually **never leave** the brain, he created the golden rule of habit change in a very simple formula. At the **core** is the desired goal, and first in coaching we need to ensure that the goal is clear and verbalized. Then there is the **cue**, the trigger that leads to an action. Then a **routine** takes over, which leads to the desired **reward**. This reinforces responsiveness to the cue the next time it happens. An undeniable, irresistible feedback loop in the brain is formed.

Duhigg finds that that embedding a new habit depended upon replacing the existing routine with a different routine, bookended by the two familiar aspects, the **cue** and the **reward**. When coaching the desired attainment of a new behavior or action that requires a driving change from the familiar to the unknown, the process of changing the routine appeals to brain function and is highly effective.

Coaches are the change catalysts and agents, as they support the deeply challenging emotional aspects of change by enabling the hardwiring of new learning through insight and action.

Change and the Brain

The challenge for leaders is to apply what we know about the natural function of the brain to build the full engagement needed to master the transition to a new future state.[20] The drivers that satisfy the natural inclination of the brain include communication of a meaningful mission, a positive values-based culture, the potential for opportunity and growth, support and trust, esteem and respect, interaction and rapport, and social networks that foster connections and produce wide-ranging positive dividends. In this environment, the ability to adapt, and embrace change is possible. Without this foundation, the demands

[19] Charles Duhigg, *The Power of Habit: Why we do what we do and how to change,* rh books, 2012.
[20] William Bridges, Susan Bridges, *Managing Transitions: Making the Most of Change,* Da Capo Press, 2009.

for innovation and creativity to address the sweeping changes of the twenty-first century generate only confusion, cognitive dissonance, and disengagement.

Resources for Exploration and Learning

These resources will help you to further understand the brain research behind these concepts and also guide you to apply these capabilities in your life and work.

Recommended Books

Drive: The Surprising Truth About What Motivates Us, Daniel H. Pink, Canongate Books Ltd., 2009
   o   A completely new paradigm for deep and enduring 'intrinsic' motivation derived from brain science and applied to work and life.

The Power of Habit: Why we do what we do and how to change, Charles Duhigg, rh books, 2012
   o   Provides a process and plan based on brain research to break old habits of thought and action for individuals and organizations and drive adaptation to change.

Your Brain and Business: The Neuroscience of Great Leaders, Srinivasan S. Pillay, FT Press 2011
   o   A practical approach to understanding the minds of leaders based on brain research and offering alternative coaching practices based on this data to attain high performance.

Mind-set the New Psychology of Success, Carol Dweck, Ballantine Books, 2008
   o   A science-based explanation of the limitations of a 'fixed' mind-set versus the power of the 'growth' mind-set to gain resilience, high achievement and self-esteem.

Resonant Leadership: Renewing Yourself and Connecting with Others Through Mindfulness, Hope, and Compassion, Richard Boyatsis, Annie McKee, Harvard Business School Publishing, 2005
   o   A framework drawn from multidisciplinary research that gives real-life examples and practices to build the resonance that is the identifying mark of great leaders.

Hardwiring Happiness: The New Brain Science of Contentment, Calm and Confidence, Rick Hanson, Harmony Books, 2013
- o Based on neuroscience, the practice and impact of building inner strengths of happiness, and peace, along with a compelling view on why this an important key to successful work and life.

The Other 90%: How to Unlock Your Vast Untapped Potential for Leadership and Life, Robert K. Cooper, Three Rivers Press, 2001
- o How to harness your brain – head, heart, gut – the 90 percent of our capacity and brainpower that in most people is dormant.

Brain Changer: How Harnessing Your Brain's Power to Adapt Can Change Your Life, David DiSalvo, BenBella Books, 2013
- o Drawing from the fields of cognitive psychology, neuroscience, behavioral economics, and communication, practical steps are given to change thinking and lives.

Assessment and Videos

ASSESSMENT	URL	QR CODE IMAGE
01	**TEST YOUR MIND-SET** http://mind-setonline.com/testyourmind-set/step1.php Offered by Carol Dweck, you can test your current mind-set whether 'fixed' or 'growth' oriented Tiny URL: **http://tinyurl.com/38psn6p**	
VIDEOS		
02	Dan Pink, **The Puzzle of Motivation**, TED talk http://www.ted.com/talks/dan_pink_on_motivation?language=en Tiny URL: **http://tinyurl.com/lx75scy**	
03	Richard Boyatsis, **Power of Resonant Leadership** http://www.youtube.com/watch?v=_ReerNT2VMA Tiny URL: **http://tinyurl.com/klgbdg9**	

CHAPTER 2

Pursuing Optimism and Positivity

Purpose and Outcomes

The purpose of this chapter is to explore the new field of positive psychology and uncover the impact that optimism and positivity can have on leading a productive, healthy, and rewarding life.

The insights will enable you to:

- acquire flexible resilience in the face of barriers, adversity, and failure
- realistically evaluate problems and reframe difficulties as opportunities
- replace toxic self-talk with an affirmative explanatory style
- find creative solutions in uncertain economic or organizational turbulence
- inspire optimism in others

Before his death in 2008, Randy Pausch, a Carnegie Mellon professor of computer science, chose to reveal his terminal cancer in a now famous lecture that later became the title of a book about his life – *The Last Lecture*. The Last Lecture is a tradition at Carnegie Mellon and it is the lecture offered each year by a different faculty member, who gives the lecture as if it were the last one of his life. Ironically, Randy had been selected to deliver this lecture before he found out that he had terminal cancer.

What could have been a dreary, morbid experience became a hopeful and humorous presentation. Finding positive meaning and purpose in his illness and mortality, Randy chose to inspire others to pursue their childhood dreams. His mission was to encourage all, especially his children, to embrace life with acceptance of what is. He wanted everyone to strive for what can be, regardless of what happens. With resilience and optimism, Pausch said, *"We cannot change the cards we are dealt, just how we will play the hand."*[21]

> **What the caterpillar calls a tragedy, the Master calls a butterfly.**
> ∞Richard Bach, author of *Jonathan Livingston Seagull*

Optimism as a Positive Force in Change

Finding positivity in something as final as dying is no mean feat. For many, it's hard to stay optimistic in much less dire circumstances than Randy's.

Any kind of change is a challenge, whether negative or positive, personal or professional, by choice or imposed. It's painful to change. It's uncomfortable, and it's difficult. It requires that we move away from the familiar to the unknown – with all of its perceived dangers.

Pessimists react to change with the view that it cannot possibly be good, while optimists actively seek the benefits of change, knowing that there is a silver lining. This difference in attitude actually becomes a self-fulfilling prophecy because to a large degree, our inner thoughts create the future.

The question, then, is: *"Are optimists born that way, or is it a learned behavior?"* According to the experts, the answer is **both**. Research on identical and fraternal twins shows that the level of optimism in identical twins who are raised separately is pretty much equal. This is not true of fraternal twins, who do not share identical DNA.

According to researcher Martin Seligman – former president of the American Psychological Association, Professor of Psychology at the University of Pennsylvania, and one of the founders of the field of positive psychology – *"Roughly 50 percent of almost every personality trait turns out to be attributable to genetic inheritance."*[22] So, your level of optimism or pessimism is embedded in your DNA to some degree.

---

[21] Randy Pausch, *The Last Lecture.*
[22] Martin E.P. Seligman, *Authentic Happiness,* Free Press 2002, pg. 47.

But what about the remaining 50 percent? Fortunately, research conducted during the past 20 years has shown that optimism is a strength that can be **learned**. It can turn our minds from negative rumination, catastrophizing, and despair toward positivity, hope, and happiness – especially useful when we are in the midst of change.

What is Optimism?

The root word of optimism is from Latin optimus, meaning the best – the superlative of good. Essentially, it's the tendency to have confidence in the future. It is a mental attitude or world view that interprets situations and circumstances in an upbeat light, with future benefits and opportunities. Optimists expect the best possible outcome even if it isn't likely to happen.

Optimism inspires us, energizes peak performance, and brings out the best in individuals, teams, and organizations. It gives those who possess it a hidden competitive advantage in their professional careers and personal lives.

Explanatory Styles

As a psychologist, Seligman was trained to conduct research on mental illness – investigating what makes people feel depressed, helpless, and unable or unwilling to get out of despair. After a few decades of pursuing this perspective, however, he decided that not enough attention was being paid to what made people well, strong, and able to keep going with confidence and hope in even the most difficult of conditions.

In his pursuit Seligman found good reasons to focus on optimism. He found that optimistic people tend to live longer, earn more over a lifetime, have better health and relationships, enjoy more success at work and in school, and win more at sports.

Seligman also found that the key to understanding the thought process that drives optimism and pessimism are very different. Optimists and pessimists have very different *explanatory styles* – or, how they tell themselves the story of their experiences, whether good or bad.

The Nuns' Story

Interestingly, a longitudinal study of nuns found that their autobiographies, written in 1932 when they were novices in the School Sisters of Notre Dame, had very different emotional styles.

Sister 1 (low positive emotion): "*I was born on September 26, 1909, the eldest of seven children, five girls and two boys...My candidate year was spent in the Motherhouse, teaching Chemistry and Second Year Latin at Notre Dame Institute. With God's grace, I intend to do my best for our Order, for the spread of religion and for my personal sanctification.*"

Sister 2 (high positive emotion): "*God started my life off well by bestowing upon me a grace of inestimable value....The past year which I have spent as a candidate studying at Notre Dame College has been a very happy one. Now I look forward with eager joy to receiving the Holy Habit of Our Lady and to a life of union with Love Divine.*"

The study of all 180 nuns revealed over their lives that those with an optimistic and positive explanatory style lived longer – 90 percent of the most cheerful were still alive at age 85, as opposed to only 34 percent of the least positive. And further along, 54 percent of the happy nuns were alive at age 94, whereas only 11 percent of the more pessimistic nuns still lived.[23]

Seligman defines these explanatory styles as having three dimensions: permanence, pervasiveness, and personalization.[24]

When something bad happens to optimists, they tell themselves that their troubles are transient, controllable, and specific to that one situation. They put the bad experience in a box with a strong padlock.

When something bad happens to pessimists, they tell themselves that their troubles are permanent, due to personal failures, and likely to recur in all facets of their lives. The *badness* has no boundaries in the mind of the pessimist, who believes that he/she personally caused it to happen.

---

[23] D. Danner, D. Snowden, W. Friesen, Positive Emotions In Early Life and Longevity, Findings from the Nun Study, Journal of Personality and Social Psychology, 2001, Vol. 80, No. 5, 804-813.

[24] Martin E.P. Seligman, *Learned Optimism: How to Change Your Mind and Your Life*, Vintage, 2006, pp. 31-53.

PERMANCE	OPTIMIST BELIEVES	PESSIMIST BELIEVES
GOOD EVENT	Last Forever	Brief, Short Lived
BAD EVENT	Brief, Short Lived	Last Forever

PERVASIVENESS	OPTIMIST BELIEVES	PESSIMIST BELIEVES
GOOD EVENT	Spread Through Whole Life	Limited To This Event
BAD EVENT	Limited To This Event	Spread Through Whole Life

PERSONALIZATION	OPTIMIST BELIEVES	PESSIMIST BELIEVES
GOOD EVENT	I Made This Happen	Luck Or Chance
BAD EVENT	Luck Or Chance	I Made This Happen

However, when good things happen, this explanatory style turns on its head. Optimists tell themselves that this good thing will have a permanent impact on their lives (permanence), will spread out into multiple facets of their experience (pervasiveness), and was directly due to their actions (personalization).

Pessimists again follow the opposite path in telling themselves that the good thing is temporary (permanence), is limited to that one time and circumstance (pervasiveness), and was the result of something outside their control (personalization). Because of their thought processes, optimists create the conditions for a bright future, while pessimists pave the way for hopelessness and helplessness.

Optimists take a failure or bad event in stride and don't allow it to gain the upper hand. They look at it as a temporary setback, holding to the belief that the future holds brighter promises. Optimists also reflect on the good experiences in their lives with gratitude and thankfulness. They believe that nothing can hinder their success in reaching their goals, and, like Randy Pausch, they find meaning and purpose even in adversity.

Another interesting discovery was that Seligman reviewed the explanatory style of candidates for president of the United States from 1948 to 1984, and he found that in every case, voters chose an optimistic leader rather than a pessimistic one.[25]

---

[25] Martin E.P. Seligman, *Learned Optimism: How to Change Your Mind and Your Life*, Vintage, 2006 pgs. 185 – 197.

Building the propensity for an optimistic explanatory style is important to a life well lived!

Acquiring the Mind of the Optimist

We can see that optimism is an essential trait of great leaders and most especially, entrepreneurs.

In 1968, at a time when the U.S. economy was in disrepair, the Vietnam War was generating riots and protests, and Robert F. Kennedy and Martin Luther King were assassinated, Robert Noyes and his partners founded Intel. Others might have believed the chaos and confusion in that time posed a detriment to a startup venture, but not Noyes. He states that optimism is: *"an essential ingredient of innovation. How else can the individual embrace change over security, adventure over staying in safe places?"*

However, all of us – even optimists – have negative thoughts and self-doubt at times, no matter how naturally optimistic and positive we may be. The good news is that Seligman and other researchers have found that the brain can be reprogrammed to dispute a negative thought, defeating it before it takes root. This means that once you become aware of your thought patterns, you can recognize the negative phrases or sentences within your distorted self-talk and reframe them before they destroy your self-confidence, discount your strengths, or turn you against yourself.

> **Whether you think you can or think you can't. You are right.**
> ∞Henry Ford, founder of Ford Motor Company

In neuroscience, this is called *metacognition* – the ability of your brain to think, while at the same time, thinking about what you are thinking. It's a powerful tool that can make you self-aware and liberate you from robotic repetition in your thought processes. You can learn to interrupt a negative thought and replace it with a different, positive one, or you can postpone thinking about the negative thought at all.

Researchers have also discovered that if you want to acquire a new state of mind, it's a good idea to change your behavior first. When you act as if you're an optimist, the new mind-set will follow. Apparently, the brain cannot tell the difference between real or fake optimistic smiles, calm breathing, positive body language, and upbeat speech. Your brain simply follows the signals your body sends it. So, even performing the *behaviors* of an optimist leads to positive habits in the mind.

Optimism and Resiliency

Resilience is both the quality of a material to resume its original shape after being stretched, bent, or compressed, **and** the similar ability in humans to recover quickly from illness, change, or misfortune.[26] Optimistic people are resilient and persevere when others would give up. They are not Pollyannas, deluding themselves with positivity. They just release negative thoughts and refuse to ruminate about a failure, loss, or problem. Instead, they quickly shift their attention to the positive potential or opportunity inherent in the circumstance.

Malala's Story

In 2012 at the age of 14, Malala Yousafzai was shot in the head by the Taliban. She had been writing an honest and courageous blog about her challenges and difficulties in defying the Taliban ban on education for girls in Pakistan. The Taliban wanted to silence her voice. This could have defeated a pessimist, but Malala survived and more importantly she has acquired an even a stronger and more positive voice in the fight for the rights of girls to have an education. She has become the global face for girls' education and is the youngest person to be awarded the Nobel Peace Prize.

"I told myself, Malala, you have already faced death. This is your second life. Don't be afraid — if you are afraid, you can't move forward."

Teams and organizations also have the ability to build optimism and positivity, and it's critical for leaders to develop it, first in themselves and then foster it on their teams.

Barbara Fredrickson, Kenan Distinguished Professor of Psychology at the University of North Carolina, has found that to maintain positivity

---

[26] The Free Dictionary by Farlex.

in the midst of difficult experience, you must dispute your own negative thinking. She doesn't suggest suppressing or white-washing these thoughts, but conducting a reality check on any depressing interpretation and projection of events.[27]

Two of her theories are especially helpful in developing a positive rather than a negative bias in the brain:

- **Three to One Ratio** – This concept is derived from mathematics, where a ratio defines how much of one thing is equivalent to another thing. Fredrickson finds that the positivity to negativity ratio must be three heartfelt positive thoughts/emotions/experiences to each heart wrenching negative one. This is related to the process described in Chapter 1: The Neuroscience of Leading Change, and occurs when we access and use self-directed neuroplasticity to deepen the positive rather than the negative neural pathways.
- **Broaden and Build** –This is the theory that positive emotions open people's minds to possibility, creativity, opportunity *broadening and building* capability, in contrast to negative emotions which narrow and limit the mind.

Another helpful tool to counter your negative ruminations comes from Chris Argyris' work – the *Ladder of Inference*.[28] The Ladder of Inference shows us how we create meaning from our own belief structures as we observe the behaviors, actions, and words of others – in other words, how we tell the stories inside our heads. The ladder of inference offers insights into a *completely normal* thought process, which all humans must follow in order to gather, select, and explain behavioral data. This process can lead to actions we take, based on the *stories* we create.

---

[27] Barbara Frederickson, *Positivity: Top-Notch Research Reveals the 3 –to – 1 Ratio That Will Change Your Life*, Three Rivers Press, 2009, pp 159-163.

[28] R. Ross, The Ladder of Inference, in P. Senge, A. Kliener, C. Roberts, R. Ross, & B. Smith. *The fifth discipline fieldbook; Strategies and tools for building a learning organization*. New York: Doubleday, 1994, pp. 242-246.

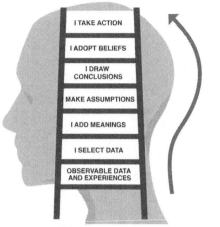

Ladder of Inference, Chris Argyris – Source: The Fifth Discipline, Peter Senge, 1994

However, if you climb the ladder of inference unconsciously and access only your individual filters to create your story, you run the risk of misinterpreting the true meaning of other people's behavior. The danger of misinterpretation lies especially in the steps on the ladder of:

- I add meanings
- I make assumptions
- I draw conclusions

And this misinterpretation when fed by the natural negative bias of the brain could lead you to take inappropriate actions.

The Ladder of Inference in Action

A woman from the United States was walking down the street in a developing world country and saw a man leading a small child by the hand. A dog approached the man and the child. Immediately, the man snatched up the child and kicked the dog away. The woman, who loved animals, ran quickly up the Ladder of Inference and decided that this was a bad man guilty of cruelty to animals. When in reality, if she had checked in with him on his actions, he would have told her that it was a stray dog and could carry diseases that would harm his child.

If you're aware of the progressive steps on the ladder of inference, and remain conscious of your filters as you take those steps, you can stop yourself from racing up the ladder based on misunderstandings, false assumptions, or incorrect data. And you can dispute the tendency toward negative thinking. Of course, as noted in Chapter 4: Generating Emotional and Social Intelligence, leaders have a special responsibility to challenge negative thinking in themselves and on their teams.

Making Optimism a Way of Life

The research has shown that there is more benefit in being an optimist than a pessimist. Optimists experience less distress under difficult circumstances, continue their efforts in the face of adversity, leverage more effective coping strategies, and follow behaviors that promote physical and mental health – leading to more satisfying lives, relationships, and careers.

> *I am an optimist. It does not seem too much use being anything else.*
> ∞Winston Churchill, British Statesman and Prime Minister

So, when you face a situation with the potential of a serious negative outcome, it makes sense to conduct a cautious risk assessment. Seligman proposes applying *flexible optimism* in your life, utilizing a pessimistic mind-set when necessary but with the wisdom to recognize when a pessimistic **bias** is blockading your ability to act positively.

This is not an easy path to take, but we become better at it with experience.

Resources for Exploration and Learning

The following resources have been carefully selected to help you to build your optimism and positivity, always balancing this outlook with a realistic assessment of risk and problems, but learning not to become stuck in negative thoughts and emotions.

On the Internet are several tools for you to assess your Optimism Quotient, your Positivity Ratio, and how happy you are at work. Once armed with this self-awareness you can pursue learning more about building optimism and positivity for yourself and your organization by reading the recommended books and watching the online videos.

Recommended Books

Learned Optimism: How to Change Your Mind and Your Life, Martin E.P. Seligman, Vintage 2006
- o   On pages 32 – 51 there is an assessment for you to evaluate your explanatory style, whether pessimistic or optimistic on the three dimensions – permanence, pervasiveness, and personalization.
- o   Also, Chapter 13, *'Helping Your Child Escape Pessimism'*, gives excellent recommendations to build optimism during childhood.

Authentic Happiness, Martin E.P. Seligman, Free Press 2002
- o   A discussion of benefits of happiness and a formula to assess your happiness level.

Hard Optimism, Price Pritchett, Pritchett LLP 2004
- o   Tips and techniques to develop deep strengths for managing uncertainty, opportunity, adversity, and change.

Resilience: The Power to Bounce Back When the Going Gets Tough!, Frederic Flach, MD, Hatherleigh Press 1997
- o   Describes the 14 traits that will make you more resilient and the process of reframing your problem so that you can create a life you can enjoy.

Positivity: Top-Notch Research Reveals the 3 – to – 1 Ratio That Will Change Your Life, Barbara L. Frederickson, Three Rivers Press 2009
- o   Frederickson describes how experiencing positive emotions broadens people's minds and builds their resourcefulness. Applying the suggestions enables you to be more resilient to adversity and effortlessly achieve what you once could only imagine.

Assessments and Meditations

ASSESSMENT	URL	QR CODE IMAGE
04	**Optimism Assessment** adapted from Martin Seligman's work on Learned Optimism http://www.stanford.edu/class/msande271/onlinetools/LearnedOpt.html Tiny URL: **http://tinyurl.com/y9u422**	
05	**Positivity Ratio Assessment** http://www.positivityratio.com/single.php Tiny URL: **http://tinyurl.com/dl43zu**	
06	**Happiness at Work Assessment** https://www.happinessatworksurvey.com/ Tiny URL: **http://tinyurl.com/pep47zd**	
MEDITATION	*To build optimism and positivity*	
07	**Positivity Meditations** http://www.positivityresonance.com/meditations.html Tiny URL: **http://tinyurl.com/n8a8a78**	
08	**Positivity Meditation** video http://www.youtube.com/watch?v=sz7cpV7ERsM&feature=related Tiny URL: **http://tinyurl.com/lll3g8g**	
VIDEOS		
09	**Positivity Resonates,** Barbara Frederickson http://rossmedia.bus.umich.edu/rossmedia/Play/2a9ecfd04942483591fad7d0800cb82b1d Tiny URL: **http://tinyurl.com/lq3p85z**	
10	**The Last Lecture,** Randy Pausch http://www.youtube.com/watch?v=ji5_MqicxSo Tiny URL: **http://tinyurl.com/2z3wsx**	

CHAPTER 3

Practicing Mindfulness

Purpose and Outcomes

The purpose of this chapter is to explore the value of mindfulness practices and demonstrate the relationship of mindfulness to:
- increased self-awareness and self-management, fostering less emotional reactivity
- improved mental focus
- openness to new ideas and creative solutions
- expressing compassion and empathy for self and others

Early one morning in a Washington, DC Metro station, a man with a violin played six Bach pieces for about 45 minutes. Of 1,097 people who walked by on their way to work, only seven stopped and listened for a short while. Twenty more gave money but continued to walk at their normal pace. The man collected a total of $32.17. When he finished playing, silence took over. No one noticed, and no one applauded. There was no recognition at all.

The passersby didn't know this, but the violinist was Joshua Bell, one of the greatest musicians in the world. He played one of the most intricate pieces ever written, with a violin crafted in 1713 and worth $3.5 million dollars. Two days before, Joshua had sold-out a theater in Boston where people paid an average of $100 each to sit and listen to him play the same music.

This is a true story of an event organized by *The Washington Post*. Joshua Bell, playing incognito in the D.C. Metro station, was there as part of a social experiment about perception, taste, and priorities. The question they explored was: "*In a routine environment at an inappropriate hour, do we perceive beauty? If so, do we stop to appreciate it? Do we recognize talent in an unexpected context?"*

The Metro riders demonstrated that we do not. If we don't have a moment to stop and listen to one of the best musicians in the world playing some of the finest music ever written with one of the most beautiful instruments ever made: *"How many other things do we miss as we mindlessly rush through life?"*[29]

Mindfulness as a Positive Force in Change

The practice of mindfulness focuses on the present moment as the only moment of life we actually possess, as the past is gone, and the future has not yet arrived. Mindfulness helps us accept life as an emergent process of change and develop the psychological flexibility to create an active and watchful mind that is curious and open.

While it began as a meditation technique practiced outside of corporate atmospheres, mindfulness is increasingly now being employed by leaders and executives to improve their work performance. To be effective in leading change in turbulent times– a given in the twenty-first century – leaders need to acquire and maintain a calm and open mind.

Executives who practice mindfulness cultivate the ability to focus attention, reduce stress, build more self-awareness and empathy, become better listeners, readily recognize their intuition, and adapt to change more rapidly than others. These leaders create a culture of connection, openness, and balance.

In my experience, mindful people make much better leaders than frenetic, aggressive ones. They understand their reactions to stress and crises, and understand their impact on others. They are far better at inspiring people to take on greater responsibilities and at aligning them around common missions and values. They are better at focusing and are more effective at delegating work with closed-loop follow-up. As a result,

---

[29] Gene Weingarten, "Pearls Before Breakfast," *The Washington Post*, April 8, 2007, http://www.washingtonpost.com/wp-dyn/content/article/2007/04/04/AR2007040401721.html (accessed April 2, 2014).(Tiny URL: http://tinyurl.com/32a32w)

people follow their mindful approach, and their organizations outperform others over the long-run.
∞Bill George, former CEO of Medtronics and currently a professor at Harvard Business School.[30] Bill George has been practicing mindful meditation for 40 years.

What is Mindfulness?

The most succinct and relevant definition comes from one of the founders of mindfulness practice in modern times, Jon Kabat-Zinn, who defines it as: *"Paying attention in a particular way: on purpose, in the present moment, and non-judgmentally."*[31]
Mindfulness is about becoming awake and conscious of the fullness of each moment of life, helping us to navigate the constant change and stresses in our lives, which are increasing with ever more complexity and disruption.

Is Multi-Tasking Mindful?

The twenty-first century is an era of globalization and rapid technological change, which is described by the U.S. Military Academy as VUCA – A world of **V**olatility, **U**ncertainty, **C**omplexity, and **A**mbiguity. In this VUCA world, the demands on our attention are increasingly varied, dynamic, and multifaceted. Every ping of a text message, every email from a friend on Facebook who is looking for you, every feed on your computer, every post to Instagram or Twitter is another in the unceasing stream of interruptions. Yet, the belief is that we can do all of this while simultaneously writing a report, coding software, or cooking a meal.

We call it multi-tasking, believing that the ability to do this well increases our productivity. The concept of multi-tasking was derived from the world of computers, where parallel processing has been in operation for decades. Then, when we were confronted with the VUCA world of demands and complexity accompanied by the growth of a multitude of

---

[30] Bill George, "Resilience Through Mindfulness Practice," *Huffington Post,* March 22, 2013 http://www.huffingtonpost.com/bill-george/resilience-through-mindfu_b_2932269.html (accessed April 2, 2014). (Tiny URL: http://tinyurl.com/ara7vfj)
[31] Jon Kabat-Zinn, *Wherever You Go, There You Are: Mindfulness Meditation in Everyday Life,* New York: Hyperion, 1994.

technologies, we adopted the concept for humans. The modern world believes it's possible and even desirable for humans to complete several unrelated tasks simultaneously.

This has involved us in the *busy-ness* of business. We become *humans doing* rather than *human beings* and with unfortunate consequences.

Multi-tasking has been proven to be a persistent modern myth. Neuroscience has shown through recent brain research that there are two negative outcomes when we jump from task to task. The brain is a linear, single processor, truly capable of only one thing at a time. When we are multi-tasking, we can't devote our attention to any one thing and we sacrifice the quality of our attention. Additionally, work takes more time (It takes 50 percent more time to complete a task when it is interrupted), and we commit more errors.

The Benefits of Mindfulness

Recent research by Clifford Nass, a psychology professor at Stanford University (along with research by others with similar findings), shows that multi-taskers are 40 percent less productive and that multi-tasking limits our ability to concentrate, analyze, and feel empathy.[32] Multi-tasking also generates cortisol, which is the stress hormone that causes memory dysfunction and high blood pressure, among other negative effects.

A study in the UK found that 86 percent of people agreed that they *"would be much happer and healthier if they knew how to slow down and live in the moment."* (*Be Mindful Report*, Mental Health Foundation 2010)

> **Yesterday is history. Tomorrow is a mystery. Today is a gift – that is why they call it the Present.**
> ∞ Original author unknown

Multiple research studies around the world have assessed the impact of mindfulness meditation on managing stress and focusing the mind, and the results are powerful. The benefits in overall health, well-being, and productivity are so compelling that a variety of Fortune 500 companies – including Ford Motor Company, McKinsey & Co, Google, Aetna International, Monsanto, Raytheon, Proctor & Gamble, General

---

[32] E. Ophir, C. Nass,, A. Wagner, Cognitive Control in Media Multitaskers, *Proceedings of the National Academy of Sciences,* August 24, 2009.

Mills, Comcast, BASF, Unilever, and Nortel Networks – are providing mindfulness training for their employees.

During the meeting of world leaders at the Davos World Economic Forum 2013, Janice Marturano, a General Mills attorney for 15 years before retiring in 2012, presented the *Mindful Leader Experience* with Oxford University Professor Mark Williams to a packed audience of executives from around the world. Janice believes that the capability of the mind, like the body, can be developed through exercise and that the more people multi-task, the less efficient and creative they are at completing a task or solving complex problems. Since her retirement, she has created the Institute for Mindful Leadership, and thousands of executives from General Mills, Medtronics, Proctor & Gamble, and the US military have been trained in this mindfulness practice.

Mindfulness cultivates our ability to sustain attention for longer periods of time – to be in the moment in order to make clear decisions.[33]
∞ Janice Marturano, Institute for Mindful Leadership

This is fully depicted in the Chinese character for mindfulness:

**Chinese character
for Mindfulness:
Presence + Heart**

The state of a person's mind affects the body on a physical level as well. Harvard Medical School research demonstrates that stress has serious

---

[33] Grant Moos, "'Mindful Leadership' debuts at World Economic Forum," *Taste of General Mills*, January 23, 2012 http://blog.generalmills.com/2013/01/mindful-leadership-debuts-at-world-economic-forum/ (accessed April 2, 2014). (Tiny URL: http://tinyurl.com/q4pwtsq)

negative effects on the body linked to heart rate and high blood pressure, weakened immunity, and lower fertility. Mindful mediation has exactly the opposite impact – lowering blood pressure, improving digestion, and boosting immunity.

In 1981, Ellen Langer, a pioneer in mindfulness, was beginning her career at Harvard. With her colleagues, she designed a study of the power of a focused mind. They gathered 22 men in their 70s and 80s, and took them to a monastery. The first group of men were asked to act as if it were 1959, when they were young. The second group was asked only to reminisce about that era. The researchers enhanced the experience by providing items from that time – 1950s issues of *Life* magazine and the *Saturday Evening Post*, a black-and-white television, and a vintage radio.

After just one week, there were dramatic positive changes. The results of cognitive and physical tests before and after the week's experience indicated that both groups were stronger and more flexible. There were improvements in gait (some even gave up their walking canes), height, posture, hearing and vision. Intelligence tests also showed positive improvements.

But the men who had actually **behaved** as if they were young men showed significantly more improvement than those who only reminisced. Those who had impersonated younger men seemed to have bodies that actually *were* younger. This is in harmony with what is discussed in Chapter 2: Pursuing Optimism and Positivity, that the brain actually responds to behavior, even if the behavior is not real but faked.

Langer went on to conduct many more studies on the power and benefits of mindfulness. She terms her experiments *counterclockwise*, and she certainly turned back time and biological aging for these men.

Wherever you put the mind, the body will follow.[34]
∞Ellen Langer, Harvard faculty member and researcher

Practicing mindfulness focuses and calms the mind, and has positive impacts on the human body as well.

---

[34] Cara Feinberg, "The Mindfulness Chronicles," *Harvard Magazine,* September-October 2010, http://harvardmagazine.com/2010/09/the-mindfulness-chronicles?page=all (accessed April 2, 2014). (Tiny URL: http://tinyurl.com/d4f3aqm)

Mindfulness Meditation

We deal daily with extraordinary stresses of volatility, uncertainty, complexity, and ambiguity, the VUCA world described earlier. This can cause the amygdala portion of the brain to lock into a constant hyper-vigilant state and drives it to react quickly in *flight or fight* mode. The amygdala can kick in when you receive an angry email, whenever you get cut-off in traffic, or feel disrespected by a colleague. When the uncontrolled amygdala takes over, it shuts down the pre-frontal cortex of the brain, which is the seat of logical thought and judgment. This creates those moments when you do or say things that cause you to later ask yourself, *"What was I thinking?"*

You actually weren't thinking at all. The amygdala-driven mind focuses on the immediate problem and takes action based on emotions alone, not the strategic problem-solving that requires both thought and emotion. (See the Chapter 4: Generating Emotional and Social Intelligence).

A Successful Mindfulness Course

Chade-Meng Tan, a software engineer and employee #107 at Google, worked on engineering projects for eight years during the launch of Google. Then, he became the Head of Personal Growth. While in that position, Meng and his team recognized the stress their colleagues were under and the impact of that stress on the Google culture. In response they created a mindfulness-based emotional intelligence curriculum, called *Search Inside Yourself*. The intent was to enable Google employees to better manage the stress and speed required from them in their work.

The course has three steps: attention training, self-knowledge and self-mastery, and the creation of useful mental habits. It includes challenging topics such as joy independent of pleasure and meditative practices for developing kindness and compassion. One tool the course teaches is S.B.N.R.R. — nicknamed the Siberian North Railroad but actually short for *Stop, Breathe, Notice, Reflect and Respond*, a sure protection against an amygdala or emotional hijacking, as this provides a mindful method to engage the whole brain and the body in deciding what to do next.

Thousands of Google employees have taken the program, and it's always fully subscribed. The rating is consistently 4.75 out of 5 in terms of appreciation for its value.

Mindfulness meditation helps you to slow down the negative reactivity of the amygdala. It isn't just a process of changing your mind; neuroplasticity, a process of growth in grey matter even in a mature brain, allows changes in the structure and function of your brain to what you attend. If you alter what you think, do, and pay attention to, your brain changes.

Advances in neuroscience and psychology over the past 15 years have demonstrated that mindfulness practice benefits us by:

1. Decreasing the grey matter in the amygdala (the fight or flight mechanism in the brain) and levels of the stress hormone, cortisol.
2. Increasing the grey matter in the areas of the brain associated with attention, memory, and empathy – the medulla oblongata that controls autonomic functions such as breathing, digestion, heart and blood vessel functions.[35]

So, when you practice mindfulness meditation, you calm and quiet your mind, gain awareness of your emotions and thoughts, and acquire self-mastery. By flexing the *muscles* of your mind, you strengthen your attention and focus. You become more receptive and upbeat, and you experience pleasure in the present moment. Most importantly, you recognize the habitual patterns of your mind and adopt a *beginner's mind* that permits you to look at experiences as if for the first time. This process creates new response patterns that drive innovation and creativity.

In the beginner's mind there are many possibilities; in the expert's mind there are few.
∞Shunryu Suzuki, Zen monk and teacher

---

[35] Massachusetts General Hospital, "Mindfulness meditation training changes brain structure in 8 weeks," http://www.massgeneral.org/about/pressrelease.aspx?id=1329 (accessed April 2, 2014). (Tiny URL: http://tinyurl.com/4nznn9c)

Practicing Mindfulness

You will realize the benefits of mindfulness in the first week that you practice the meditation technique. With just ten minutes a day for ten days, you will awaken to your experience moment-by-moment in the present. You will also acquire the foundation needed to observe your thoughts and feelings from a distance, non-judgmentally, and you will regard your experiences with more openness, interest, and curiosity.

The good news is that mindfulness meditation can be practiced anywhere, anytime – even in the midst of a stressful meeting. Those who practice it can shift on demand to an attentive mental state, amplifying self-awareness and self-management. Compassion and empathy are also increased as we accept – without judgment – all of the inescapable imperfections that arise in ourselves, in others, and in situations we encounter on the job and elsewhere.

Mindfulness fosters a state of greater peace that enhances not just performance, but all aspects of life, in a multi-dimensional way.

Resources for Exploration and Learning

The following selected resources will help you to begin your mindfulness practice.

Recommended Books

Mindfulness for Beginners: Reclaiming the Present Moment and Your Life, Jon Kabat-Zinn, Sounds True, Inc., 2012
  o Written in a unique way, this book is presented in chapters, each of which reflects a mindfulness practice. It includes a complete CD with five guided mindfulness meditations by Jon Kabat-Zinn.

Mindful Leadership, Maria Gonzalez, Josey-Bass, A Wiley Imprint, 2012
  o This book describes the source of true leadership, a calm and focused mind, and provides mindfulness meditation practices to achieve clarity, reduce stress and develop a focused mind.

Article, Assessments, Meditation Practices & Videos

ARTICLE	URL	QR CODE IMAGE
11	**Managing negative emotions** http://www.psychologytoday.com/files/attachments/51483/handling-the-hijack.pdf Tiny URL: **http://tinyurl.com/jvuwnnc**	
ASSESSMENT AND PRACTICE		
12	**Compassionate Organization Quiz** http://greatergood.berkeley.edu/quizzes/take_quiz/11 Tiny URL: **http://tinyurl.com/chufd4k**	
13	**Test Your Focus** http://www.nytimes.com/interactive/2010/06/07/technology/20100607-task-switching-demo.html Tiny URL: **http://tinyurl.com/36nnhee**	
14	**3 minute "Breathing Space" mindfulness meditation** http://oxfordmindfulness.org/learn/resources/ Tiny URL: **http://tinyurl.com/d26u2q8**	

15	Meditation app 10 minutes/10 days http://www.getsomeheadspace.com/ Tiny URL: **http://tinyurl.com/33arn2a**	
16	**6 Mindfulness Exercises for Those Who Don't Want to Meditate** http://www.psychologytoday.com/blog/in-practice/201302/6-mindfulness-exercises-each-take-less-1-minute Tiny URL: **http://tinyurl.com/mesclzf**	
17	**Meditations on self-compassion** http://www.mindfulselfcompassion.org/meditations_downloads.php Tiny URL: **http://tinyurl.com/b3uf43r**	
VIDEOS		
18	**Information on benefits of meditation and meditation videos** http://www.unh.edu/health-services/ohep/meditation Tiny URL: **http://tinyurl.com/nrmlmnx**	
19	**Mindfulness at Google** Chade–Meng Tan describes the impact of the highly popular program he developed for Google – *Search Inside Yourself* – with humor and relevant insights. http://www.youtube.com/watch?v=r8fcqrNO7so&feature=youtu.be Tiny URL: **http://tinyurl.com/ksm9uo5**	

CHAPTER 4

Generating Emotional and Social Intelligence

Purpose and Outcomes

This chapter describes the differentiated benefits and bottom-line results gained by individuals, teams, and organizations through the exercise of emotional and social intelligence – *the ability to access and apply knowledge and insights from personal emotions and the emotions of others to inform decisions on the best course of action.*

By generating emotional and social intelligence you have the potential to:

- relieve stress
- communicate more effectively
- exercise empathy with others
- overcome obstacles and challenges
- resolve conflicts as they arise

Based on the results of an emotional intelligence assessment, Hans, a European executive, determined to work on self-management, specifically controlling stress, reactivity and negative emotions driven by these pressures in his life. After some discussion with an executive coach on the techniques he might use, he took action. About six weeks later during the next coaching session he was eager to tell his coach about a recent positive experience.

As a hobby, he was working toward his airplane pilot license. Although all of his classmates had moved forward to their solo flight, his instructors had held him back. Then a week prior to the coaching session, they told him he could complete his solo flight, which he did successfully.

Afterward, he asked the instructors why he had been held back and they told him that it was because he had always seemed so stressed that they were worried about letting him do the solo flight. Recently, they found that he had changed and he didn't seem nearly so stressed and ready to explode. Hans attributed this change to his work on building his emotional intelligence and found his results on-the-job were also improving.

Emotional and Social Intelligence as a Positive Force in Change

The Information Age has certainly dramatically changed the nature of work. During the Industrial Age, work was divided among many workers, who didn't necessarily need to think. They could just do their small routine task in the collective endeavor. Leaders gave orders, and employees followed.

The Information Age is a different animal. Accelerating advancements in technology have allowed routine tasks to be automated or outsourced. So, the demand today is for *knowledge workers* – people who collaborate to provide their individual expertise, knowledge, and skills to the team's efforts. This type of employee requires a different relationship to their tasks, fellow workers, and employers. They want to control their own work and contributions, and they want to make personal decisions about their priorities and processes.

This change has been met by a related change in leadership styles, moving from *command and control* to an approach that promotes team harmony, stimulates high engagement, and employs coaching for teams and individuals.

This new style requires strong emotional and social skills because these capabilities enable the individual knowledge workers and their leaders to boost cooperation, build consensus, make rapid and better decisions, and drive innovation.

In order to develop these skills, organizations have begun to implement emotional intelligence assessments and training. Below are some of these organizations and the results they have experienced.

US Navy	Egon Zehnder International Executive Search firm	Major Insurance Company	L'Oreal
Characteristics of superior versus average commanders were compared, and it was found that the superior commanders were emotionally more expressive, warmer, smiled more, were friendly, appreciative, and more trustful than the average officers.	Analyzed 515 senior executives from Latin America, Germany, and Japan and found that those primarily strong in EQ skills were more successful than those with high IQ or relevant previous experience.	In the 1950s, 80 top students in scientific fields were chosen for a long-term study and given psychological and IQ tests. Forty years later, they were ranked on life success. The findings showed that emotional and social capabilities are four times more important than IQ in determining success.	New salespeople were hired based on some aspects of EQ. Then, their performance was compared with others who were hired without this consideration. The sales people chosen for EQ sold $91,370 more and had 63 percent less turnover in the first year than the control group.
Wallace Bachman: Commands in the US Navy *Nice Guys Finish First: A SYMLOG Analysis of US Naval Commands,* in Richard B. Polley et al. The SMLOG Practitioner (New York: Praeger, 1988)	Claudio Fernández-Aráoz: *Identifying emotional intelligence in job candidates,* World of Business Ideas (May 2012).	G.J.Feist and F. Barron, *Emotional Intelligence and Academic Intelligence in Career and Life Success,* paper presented to American Psychological Society (San Francisco, June 1996)	L.M. Spencer Jr. and S. Spencer, *Competence at Work: Models for Superior Performance* (New York: John Wiley and Sons, 1993)

Table 1: Enterprises Leveraging Emotional Intelligence

Why can EQ Matter More Than IQ?

Even though a high IQ is no guarantee of prosperity, prestige, or happiness in life – our schools and our culture fixate on academic abilities, ignoring the emotional intelligence that also matters immensely for our personal destiny.
∞Daniel Goleman, author, researcher, and one of the
fathers of emotional and social intelligence

The Intellectual Quotient (IQ) was popular throughout the 1900s as a test of cognitive ability. The widely held belief was that the higher your IQ, the more success you would have in life. However, a question arose in psychological circles as to whether the measure of IQ offered a complete understanding of how the mind works. Then, Howard Gardner, a psychologist at the Harvard School of Education, published *Frames of Mind: The Theory of Multiple Intelligences*, in which he proposed that the brain operates on multiple levels and employs different ways of processing information. He called this *multiple intelligences.*

Peter Salovey, who was an assistant professor in the Yale Department of Psychology at that time, was intrigued with this question: *"Why were the people with a high IQ not always the most successful in life?"* Salovey teamed up with John Mayer, a psychologist at the University of New Hampshire, and their research identified yet another of the brain's multiple intelligences, which they called *emotional intelligence* (EI), noted in their 1989 publication, *Emotional Intelligence: Imagination, Cognition and Personality.*

They developed an EI model that described high emotional competence, and they created an assessment to measure EI called the Mayer-Salovey-Caruso Emotional Intelligence Test (MSCEIT). Their model includes four major themes: Perceiving Emotions, Using Emotions, Understanding Emotions, and Managing Emotions. The format of this assessment is different from the other assessments, in that you are given a dilemma and must choose from several different options which action you would most likely take – the results of the assessment provide a real-time behavioral model that measures how *emotionally intelligent* your decisions are.

Two other major contributors to this field were Reuven BarOn, an Israeli psychologist who developed a model of emotional intelligence that he named the "Emotional Quotient (EQ),"* and Daniel Goleman, currently co-director of the Consortium for Research on Emotional Intelligence in Organizations (www.eiconsortium.org) at Rutgers University. Goleman popularized the notion of EQ in his 1996 book, *Emotional Intelligence: Why it can matter more than IQ.*[36]

Goleman introduced an EQ model and a related assessment that has four principle themes, each of which contains multiple emotional competencies. His book and assessment appealed broadly to all types of enterprises around the world – business, government, non-profit, and the military.

---

[36] Daniel Goleman, *Emotional Intelligence: Why it can matter more than IQ*, A Bantam Book, 1995.

In the Knowledge Age, as mentioned previously, an IQ that enables graduation from college and perhaps attainment of an advanced degree such as an MBA is no more than the *price of admission* to the world of work. Once employed, we're expected to work in teams, get along with people, build consensus, coach others, and thrive in change.

*In the field, EQ and EI are used interchangeably; here we will use EQ to identify this concept.

What is Emotional and Social Intelligence?

Emotional intelligence has many *fathers* and definitions. However, all of the definitions at a high level offer the view that emotional intelligence is a *neurological mental process that integrates the various parts of the brain responsible for thought and emotion to inform decision-making and action.*

Neuroscience research is proving that unlike the earlier belief that the brain was static, the brain actually changes as a result of practicing emotional intelligence, demonstrating that EQ can be learned by individuals and groups.[37] This neuroplasticity is described in a prior chapter.

Fundamentally, the concept of emotional and social intelligence is that our own emotions and the emotions of others provide critical data that we can access and manage. The most popular model of emotional intelligence used by many in the field is comprised of the recognition, identification, and management of emotions on both an individual and a social level:

- **Self-Awareness** – the capacity to recognize our emotions, distinguish among emotions, and acknowledge our intuition
- **Self-Management** – the ability to manage our emotions, especially strong, negative emotions, and control the impulses that might arise from them
- **Social Awareness** – the capacity to recognize the emotional state of others, empathetically aware of their feelings, needs, and concerns
- **Relationship Management** – the application of emotional intelligence capabilities to build strong relationships with others

---

[37] Travis Bradberry and Jean Greaves, *The Emotional Intelligence Quick Book,* Simon and Shuster 2005, pp 81 – 83.

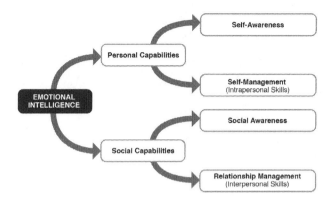

Your Brain on Emotions

Affective neuroscience is an interdisciplinary field that studies the neural processing of emotions. This science has revealed that there are four critical areas of the brain involved in recognizing, evaluating, and integrating emotions with thought:

- The **limbic system**:
  - o The **amygdala** – Comparing current experience with emotional memory, this emotional sentinel of the brain constantly evaluates the environment to determine the necessity of a *fight or flight* reaction.
  - o The **thalamus** – The air traffic controller that sends sensory data (what we see, hear, taste, touch, smell) simultaneously to the amygdala and to the cortex, the thinking brain. Unfortunately, when the danger does not require immediate *fight or flight*, the amygdala still processes the information more rapidly than the cortex, requiring only 11 milliseconds. The cortex requires 22 milliseconds, thus the need to delay and reflect on the action to be taken.

- The **cortex**:
  - o The **prefrontal cortex** – The executive center, which regulates and integrates emotions and behavior by reasoning on the consequences of our actions.
  - o The **orbitofrontal cortex** - Involved in decision-making and managing the influence of emotions on that decision.

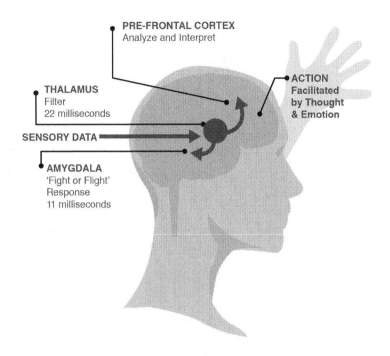

When the amygdala has a strong negative emotional reaction and the brain is not given the time to process the related fight or flight impulse through the cortex, an *amygdala or emotional hijacking* takes place. This is when you do or say something that is out of your control – something you probably regret soon after.

The Buddha and Anger

An angry young man heaped abuse on the Buddha. But the Buddha was unruffled by these insults. He remained calm, exuding a feeling of loving-kindness. He politely requested that the man come forward. Then he asked, *"Young sir, if you purchased a lovely gift for someone, but that person did not accept the gift, to whom does the gift then belong?"*

The question surprised the young man. He responded *"It would belong to me because I bought the gift."*

"That is correct," replied the Buddha. *"It is exactly the same with your anger. If I do not accept your curses, if I do not get insulted and angry in return, the anger remains yours—the same as the gift returning to its owner."*

Research has shown that negative emotions also trigger heart rhythms that are jagged and chaotic, creating chronic stress on the body and, ultimately, serious health problems and this negativity is contagious to others.[38] In his book, *Primal Leadership*, Goldman noted that the mood of the leader, whether positive or negative, is more contagious than the common cold.[39]

The Chief Executive Officer of an international pharmaceutical company told the story of when he was more junior and highly upset about something that happened at work. His boss overheard him speaking with his administrative assistant, who had no role in what had made him upset, over her cubicle wall. He walked past him saying *"You, now, in my office."* When he joined his boss in the office, the boss shut the door and said *"Your negative mood is infecting the entire office."* He told him to go into his own office, shut the door, and stay there until he had changed his attitude from negative to positive. This CEO learned a lifelong lesson he never forgot, that the leader cannot project a negative emotion. It destroys performance, motivation and energy.

> *Knowing others is intelligence; knowing yourself is true wisdom. Mastering others is strength; mastering yourself is true power.*
>
> ∞Tao Te Ching

When negative thoughts are smoothed and allowed the time needed for the sensory data to travel through the thalamus to the cortex where the amygdala's emotional response is effectively regulated – by counting to ten, for example – the cortex can override the amygdala's irrational reaction. This process allows us to take action that is facilitated by **both** thought and emotion, not just emotion alone.

Current research has also found that the heart is much more complex than previously thought and that it is in direct neurological communication

---

[38] R. McCraty, M. Atkinson, W.A. Tiller, and others. The effects of emotions on short-term heart rate variability using power spectrum analysis, *American Journal of Cardiology*, 1995, pp 76, 1089-1093.

[39] Daniel Goleman, Richard Boyatzis, Annie McKee, *Primal Leadership*, Harvard Business School Press, 2002, pp 4- 7.

with the brain. It isn't just a mechanical pump; it has an intelligence independent from the brain.[40]

In their language, many cultures recognize this two-fold role of the heart. For example, in Japanese, the word for the physical heart is *shinzu*, while the word *kokoro* refers to the *mind* of the heart. In fact, scientists have measured the electromagnetic field of the heart and found that it radiates outward eight to ten feet, but the brain only radiates outward by two feet.[41] Thus, emotional energy works at a higher speed and with greater impact than we thought.

In a May 2012 commencement address at USC's Annenberg School of Communication, Maria Schriver shared a method to manage your emotions by using the heart: *"Have the courage to press the pause button. Whenever you are in doubt, pause; take a moment, look at all your options, check your intentions, have a conversation with your heart, and then always take the high road."*

In addition by actively generating positive emotions like compassion and gratitude, we can facilitate smooth, coherent heart rhythms. And by recognizing the negative emotions and intentionally moving toward positive emotions, emotional intelligence improves.

	Relaxed	Confident	Assertive	Kind	Calm	Caring
POSITIVE EMOTIONS	Brave	Excited	Peaceful	Flexible	Healthy	Respectful
	COURAGE	SECURITY	ACCEPTANCE	TOLERANCE	HAPPINESS	LOVE
	⬆	⬆	⬆	⬆	⬆	⬆
	FEAR	ANXIETY	ANGER	FRUSTRATION	SADNESS	DISGUST
NEGATIVE EMOTIONS	Panicked	Worried	Aggressive	Annoyed	Hurt	Scornful
	Tense	Distressed	Hostile	Agitated	Depressed	Revulsed

Rather than letting negative emotions and feelings dominate in our lives with resulting increasingly detrimental behaviors, moving out of the

---

[40] Doc Childre and Howard Martin, *The Heartmath Solution*, HarperCollins, 1999, pp 28 – 34.

[41] L. Song, G. Schwartz, L. Russek, Heart-focused attention and heart-brain synchronization: Energetic and Physiological mechanisms, *Alternative Therapies in Health and Medicine*, 1998, 4(5), pp 44 - 62.

negative zone to positive emotions and thoughts, enables us to have better more fulfilling lives. If you are feeling any of the negative emotions, the antidote to this poison is the opposite positive emotion.

Recently, a young worker was completely annoyed with her supervisor. To replace feelings of scorn and revulsion, she decided to tell herself privately during conversations with this person, *"I like you and I want you to succeed"* deliberately and intentionally moving to the topline emotions. And they were amazed at how quickly the relationship turned around to one that was productive and enjoyable.

Increased EQ enables better judgment and higher productivity, enhances business and client relationships, prepares individuals to be leaders in the twenty-first century, builds more effective teams and provides an edge over the competition. [42] Emotional and social intelligence, combined with other capabilities described in this book (see Chapter 3: Practicing Mindfulness), can help control negative emotions and acquire self-mastery. By first recognizing and managing emotions, you can recognize and facilitate the emotions of others and build stronger relationships.

Finally, by leveraging the capabilities of emotional intelligence as a leader – group harmony, productivity, and cohesiveness, even in the face of great change, are built with related adaptability and flexibility in the face of challenges.

> **When dealing with people, remember you are not dealing with creatures of logic, but with creatures of emotion.**
> ∞ Dale Carnegie, writer and self-improvement guru

Resources for Exploration and Learning

The following selected resources will help you to build and leverage your own emotional and social intelligence.

---

[42] Rhonda Muir, The Importance of Emotional Intelligence in Law Firm Partners, *Law Practice Magazine*, July/August 2007 Issue, Volume 33, Number 5, pp. 60.

Recommended Books

Emotional Intelligence 2.0, Travis Bradberry and Jean Graves, TalentSmart, 2009
- o   Good introductory book that includes a code to take an EQ assessment.

Emotional Intelligence: Why it can matter more than IQ, Daniel Goleman, 1995, A Bantam Book
- o   Seminal work on how the rational and the emotional brain interact and influence our actions, decisions and behaviors.

Executive EQ: Emotional Intelligence in Leadership and Organizations, Robert Cooper and Ayman Sawaf, Berkley Publishing Group, 1996
- o   A research-based book that describes how emotional intelligence can improve any organization's success through the exercise of qualities, such as integrity, trust, and compassion, offering methods for fostering these qualities as well.

Primal Leadership: Realizing the Power of Emotional Intelligence, Daniel Goleman, Richard Boyatzis, Annie McKee, Harvard Business School Press, 2002
- o   This groundbreaking book establishes the need for leaders in the twenty-first century to master the EQ competencies of self-awareness, empathy, motivation and collaboration.

The HeartMath Solution, Doc Chidre and Howard Martin, Harpercollins, 1999
- o   Understanding the role of the heart in emotions.

Article, Assessment & Videos

ARTICLE		
20	**Controlling emotional (amygdala) hijacking** http://pd.ilt.columbia.edu/projects/exsel/aboutsel/hijack.htm Tiny URL: **http://tinyurl.com/yh6v5pd**	
ASSESSMENT		
21	**Free EQ Quiz** http://atrium.haygroup.com/us/quizzes/emotional-intelligence-quiz.aspx Tiny URL: **http://tinyurl.com/m8x7bjn**	
VIDEOS		
22	Daniel Goleman describes the **neuroscience of relationships** http://www.youtube.com/watch?v=nZskNGdP_zM&feature=related Tiny URL: **http://tinyurl.com/283gnd7**	
23	Joachim de Posada: **Don't eat the marshmallow! The importance of self-management** http://www.ted.com/talks/joachim_de_posada_says_don_t_eat_the_marshmallow_yet.html Tiny URL: **http://tinyurl.com/o6y6vg**	
24	Daniel Goleman: **Why aren't we more compassionate?** http://www.ted.com/talks/daniel_goleman_on_compassion.html Tiny URL: **http://tinyurl.com/m2r7o2**	

CHAPTER 5

Leveraging Strengths

Purpose and Outcomes

This chapter provides an introduction to strengths theory and its relevance to employee engagement, specifically how a strengths-based approach can support high engagement even through difficult change.

The insights on leveraging strengths will help you to:
- understand how to use a strengths-based approach to leadership and teaming
- explore the differences among various *strengths* assessments
- focus on building strengths rather than fixing weaknesses to yield measurable positive impacts on productivity, engagement, and results
- discover and leverage your individual and team/organizational collective strengths to drive enthusiasm and achieve high performance in life and work

Joanne – Team lead in a major company

Joanne was a high performer who always contributed to the performance of her team with her drive, eager ambition to produce excellence, and personal attention to the needs of the team members. On the team, she could be counted on to generate new and better ways of doing things, to produce strategic ideas for new initiatives, conduct in-depth research, and describe ways of integrating the team's work with a broader network of professionals in other units of the company.

The only problem was....she exhausted her team members with this effervescent spring constantly bubbling up new ideas, improvements, and initiatives. Nothing could just be accepted as good enough and repeated, even if it was successful! Frequently, she was frustrated by the seeming resistance from the team to her endless stream of ideas.

Then, she purchased StrengthsFinder® 2.0, took the StrengthsFinder® assessment from the code that is in the book, and discovered her Top 5 Signature Strengths: *Ideation, Maximizer, Strategic, Input and Relator.* As she studied the meaning of each of these strengths described in-depth in the book, she realized that she finally had a language to describe what she did with pleasure and near perfect performance every time.

However, as she explored how she was applying her strengths at work and with her team, she learned an important lesson… that any 'strength' can either be used appropriately and produce amazing benefits, or it can become a detriment when overused or used inappropriately. She understood that although she was full of ideas on how to improve everything they did together on the team, (in fact she had a new idea every 2 seconds!), not everyone was as delighted and intrigued with ideas as she was.

Now that she understood her Signature Strengths, she was no longer driven to use them at every moment and had a language to describe her signature strengths to herself and others, becoming more intentional and effective in applying her ideas when they were relevant and important.

> *I make my strengths so strong that my weaknesses become irrelevant.*
> ∞Peter Drucker, Claremont Graduate School
> professor and management guru

Strengths as a Positive Force in Change

Strengths theory and its application are strong drivers of positive change. When individuals, teams, and organizations move from a weakness-fixing performance management system to a strengths-based mind-set, there is a measurable impact on engagement, beginning an ever increasing momentum of improvements in productivity, retention, and the quality of results.

Gallup, the first originator of strengths theory, has developed a simple process enabling organizations to embed the application of strengths into their organizational DNA. There are two instruments that Gallup has developed, using their polling expertise, the StrengthsFinder® assessment that identifies individual and group strengths among 34 defined strengths and the Q12, which consists of 12 simple questions that effectively measure the engagement levels in organizations. Gallup has used these two assessments to consult with enterprises as they move toward strength-based performance processes. The outcomes have been both highly positive and measureable.

The process begins with the Q12 being completed by the organizational 'associates' (Gallup's word used to designate 'employees'). These 12 questions are have proven to be strongly related to:

- Productivity – whether the employees have the equipment and materials to do their jobs
- Well-being – the quality of employee relationships with their coworkers and managers
- Values – employee alignment with the mission of the organization

One of the questions relates directly to strengths – whether the employees have the opportunity *to do what they do best every day.* Gallup's research has found that 74 percent of employees who felt they were able to utilize their strengths in their jobs were more likely to recommend the organization's products and services. Almost 85 percent of these employees planned to be with the company one year from now, and almost 61 percent planned to spend their career there. Given the high cost of low retention, this represents a huge cost savings to organizations.[43]

This process is followed by administration of the StrengthsFinder® assessment, and the results are shared with the individuals, teams and managers. The managers are trained to use the information from the Q12. The Q12 results from their team members and direct reports are aggregated to pinpoint where improvements in their management are required. This combined with the knowledge of their direct reports Signature Strengths enables them to foster engagement, productivity and results.

---

[43] *State of the American Workplace,* Gallup, Inc., 2013, pp 21-26.

What is a Strength?

In the emerging field of positive psychology, a strength is something that you do with pleasure and near perfect performance every time. When you apply your strengths to a challenge or problem, you feel valuable and effective.

You enjoy what you're doing and want to continue the activity undistracted. Curious and alert, your mind and body are in harmony. When the task is completed, you feel satisfied and contented enough to ask, *"When can I do that again?"*

Theories About Strengths

The concept of an *optimal* experience of leveraging personal strengths to win the game is very familiar in the world of sports. When both the challenge and the ability to meet the challenge successfully are present, the best talent in individuals rises to reach the goal, and the creative energy needed to get the job done is unleashed. Sadly, people don't experience this often enough at work, and that fact leads to disengagement. (See Chapter 6: Fostering Engagement and Flow)

Decades ago, Percy Barnevik, at that time the CEO of ABB, made an interesting observation:

> *"I believe that there is a tremendous potential in our people that is not developed. Take, for example, the workers. They only use 5 to 10 percent of their brain capacity standing at a machine. Then they go home. There they administer; they organize for the children; they build a summer house. All of a sudden, they seem to be able to do an enormous amount of things. 90 to 95 percent of their brain is now at work. Now, why can't we move these people into bigger tasks?"*[44]

One answer to Barnevik's question has surfaced in a multitude of recent research studies. These have demonstrated that regardless of the signature

---

[44] Manfred Kets de Vries, *Leadership for Creativity: Generating Peak Experiences*, INSEAD Working Paper Series, 1996.

strengths used, the ability to employ strengths at work is important if we want to foster job satisfaction, pleasure, engagement, and meaning on the job.[45]

In sports the notion of playing to your strengths is common sense. Many remember the time from 1993 to 1994, when Michael Jordan retired from basketball, his strength, and joined the Chicago White Sox baseball team. As soon as the next year he rejoined the Chicago Bulls basketball team and led them to three additional championships in as well as an NBA-record of 72 regular-season wins during the 1995–96 NBA season. He returned to playing to his strengths.

Jon Montgomery – Gold Medalist, 2010 Vancouver Olympics

When Jon Montgomery was young he had big dreams of representing Canada at the Olympic Games, and especially winning a medal for his country. His first attempt to excel was by taking up hockey with the goal of getting onto the national team. Soon he found that although he was eager to learn to play the game well enough to be on the team, his ability didn't match his enthusiasm. But he didn't give up his dream to represent his country at the Winter Olympics

One day, his parents took him to watch a skeleton competition (a new, very fast sledding event that uses the same track as the luge) at the Calgary Olympic Park. Montgomery fell in love with this sport and decided this was what he wanted to do. So, he gave up playing hockey and took up learning about skeleton, using his new-found passion for this sport to push him to excel.

And after five years of playing to his strength in training and competing on the international front, Montgomery produced an 'optimal' performance and won the gold medal in skeleton at the Vancouver Games, Canada's very first medal in this event.

At last, Jon had found where he could 'play to his strengths' and could win with pleasure and near perfect performance every time.

However, in business we have unproductive theories about performance. It has been widely believed in the past that everyone can get good at everything, if they just try hard enough. Performance reviews

---

[45] *Work is more fun if the character fits the bill,* University of Zurich, MediaDesk, October 02, 2012.

represent this belief and are why everyone dislikes being involved, whether as managers or employees. The focus is usually 75 – 80 percent focused on performance deficiencies. Strengths approaches turn this theory on its head. Here the belief is that people have enduring, unique strengths and that when encouraged and aided to play to their strengths, high quality performance and full engagement result. In this method, strengths are leveraged to overcome performance deficiencies, and the questions focus on how you can utilize your strengths to address challenges.

Strengths Assessments and Tools

Four major perspectives on strengths theories and related assessments have been developed:

1. **Gallup StrengthsFinder**®, Donald Clifton and Marcus Buckingham
2. **Realise2**®, Alex Linley, Janet Willars and Robert Biswas-Diener
3. **Values in Action (VIA)**, based on the *Character Strengths and Virtues Handbook*, Christopher Peterson and Martin Seligman
4. **StandOut Leadership Strengths**, Marcus Buckingham

Gallup StrengthsFinder®

In 1952, as a graduate student in psychology, Donald O. Clifton became the *grandfather of positive psychology* when he launched the provocative notion that we should study what is strong and healthy in people rather than illness and deficiencies.

His curiosity was further peaked by interesting research, conducted in 1955 for the Nebraska School Study Council, which was focused on how to improve reading capabilities among 6,000 tenth grade students. The commonly held hypothesis at that time was that **average** readers would benefit the most from reading skills training, but the results were counterintuitive. Actually, the students who were already **above average** readers achieved exponential improvement in reading speed as a result of the training, but not the slower readers, who only demonstrated moderate improvement.

The results of this study intrigued Clifton, who went on to develop strengths theory, that if people are already excellent in doing something, investment in that ability will produce immense results.

1955 – Studied 6,000 Tenth Graders

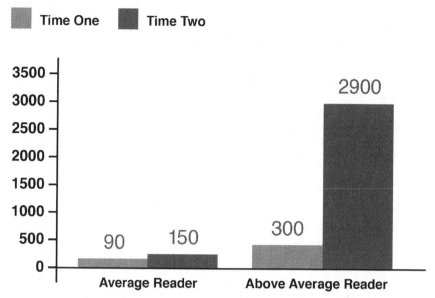

Further brain research has supported building on an investment in strengths. Studies have found that when a baby is born, there are approximately 100,000 billion neurons in the brain, each capable of 15,000 synapses. As the baby develops and learns over the next 2-3 years, there is an explosion of connections in the brain that for reasons not fully yet understood stop at about the age of three.[46] Then, a pruning work begins in the brain. The synapse connections that are used frequently become stronger like frequently traveled roadways, and unused connections disappear like a remote path in a jungle.[47]

By the time we reach our 20s, these super highways in the brain are essentially developed, widened, and paved. These highways are our enduring and unique talents and strengths. Continuing to build on this foundation with knowledge and skill further enhances our talents, and when we use our talent-based strengths we achieve success in life and work.

---

[46] Jandy Jeppson with Judith A. Myers-Walls, Dee Love, *Brain Development,*, North Carolina State University Extension Service, 1997.
[47] Jack Shonkoff, John Bruer *Adolescent Brains are a Work in Progress*, WGBH Educational Foundation, 2002.

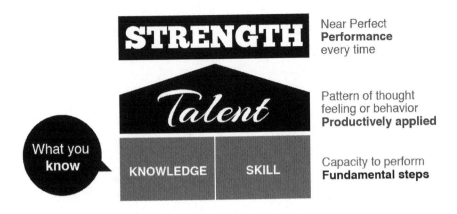

Based on these revelations, Clifton along with Marcus Buckingham used his strengths theory to develop a new assessment that could be used by individuals and organizations to identify their top five Signature Strengths. Clifton and Buckingham categorized 34 Signature Strengths themes based on the skills, knowledge, and inherent talent that people develop over a lifetime.

The Gallup StrengthsFinder® Assessment

When you take the StrengthsFinder® Assessment, you receive a report that identifies your top 5 Signature Strengths out of the 34 identified strengths. This gives you a language to understand and share how you think, where you find the most pleasure, and your greatest potential to excel in life. Once you know your strengths, you can assess whether your current work positions you to leverage them, and you now have a language to articulate your strengths to others. The appropriateness of your job in relation to your ability to employ your strengths, of course, impacts your level of engagement and your ability to achieve a sense of *flow* on the job.

This is a powerful tool that can also be used to improve team performance and determine if tasks are assigned according to the strengths of each individual. (Read more about *job sculpting* in Chapter 6: Fostering Engagement and Flow, pages 83–84.)

In the business world, Gallup has found that when managers focus on high performers and invest in building their strengths by matching those strengths to work assignments, the likelihood of success is doubled on a variety of measures. These include productivity, profitability, employee retention, customer loyalty, and safety. Success (defined as exceeding the median performance within your own company) is 86 percent greater for managers with a *strengths versus non- strengths* approach (Gallup Organization, 2002).[48] Weakness-fixing for a specific capability might be relevant if the weakness has gotten in the way of someone's overall performance, but this kind of *fixing* never supports excellence. Only an investment in strength-building does that.

Gallup's further research positioned the 34 strengths into four leadership domains.

THE FOUR DOMAINS OF LEADERSHIP*			
EXECUTING	INFLUENCING	RELATIONSHIP BUILDING	STRATEGIC THINKING
· Achiever · Arranger · Belief · Consistency · Deliberative · Discipline · Focus · Responsibility · Restorative	· Activator · Command · Communication · Competition · Maximizer · Self-Assurance · Significance · Woo	· Adaptability · Developer · Connectedness · Empathy · Harmony · Includer · Individualization · Positivity · Relator	· Analytical · Context · Futuristic · Ideation · Input · Intellection · Learner · Strategic

*Tom Rath, Barry Conchie, Strengths-based Leadership, Gallup Press, 2008

- **Executing** – strengths that can be applied to get things done
- **Influencing** – strengths that enable communication inside and outside of the organization
- **Relationship Building** – strengths that create and solidify relationships
- **Strategic Thinking** – strengths and skills that answer the important question "*Why?*"

Many organizations such as Best Buy, Ritz-Carlton Hotel Company, Standard Chartered Bank, Toyota, among others have adopted a strengths-based approach. Each of their employees take the StrengthsFinder® assessment and work with a strengths-based coach to understand how to leverage the results. Managers are trained and encouraged to *job-sculpt* people's day-to-day work to enable them to use their strengths on-the-job. Strengths coaching is revisited through the performance cycle. When managers assign a new task to their direct reports they discuss with them how they will apply their 5 Signature

---

[48] Donald Clifton, James Harter, *Investing in Strengths,* from http://media.gallup.com/ DOCUMENTS/whitePaper--InvestingInStrengths.pdf. (Tiny URL: http://tinyurl.com/ k373c9k)

Strengths to achieve success on-the-job. Performance reviews also focus not on weakness fixing, but on how strengths can be leveraged even more.

> *People don't change that much. Don't waste time trying to put in what was left out. Try to draw out what was left in. That is hard enough.*
> ∞Marcus Buckingham, the co-developer of strengths theory

CAPP® Realise2®

Another world-class assessment in the strengths field offers a more in-depth perspective on 60 strengths. Relying on the principles of building on strengths, not fixing weaknesses, the approach identifies strengths and describes methods to focus on growth and development by unlocking key strengths and minimizing areas of non-strength. These 60 strengths are assigned to 5 *Strengths Families*.

BEING			
Authenticity	Centered	Courage	Curiosity
Gratitude	Humility	Legacy	Mission
Moral Compass	Personal Responsibility	Pride	Self-Awareness
Service	Unconditionality		
COMMUNICATING			
Counterpoint	Explainer	Feedback	Humor
Listener	Narrator	Scribe	Spotlight
MOTIVATING			
Action	Adventure	Bounceback	Catalyst
Change Agent	Competitive	Drive	Efficacy
Growth	Improver	Persistence	Resilience
Work Ethic			
RELATING			
Compassion	Connector	Emotional Awareness	Empathic Connection
Enabler	Equality	Esteem Builder	Personalisation
Persuasion	Rapport Builder	Relationship Deepener	
THINKING			
Adherence	Creativity	Detail	Incubator
Innovation	Judgement	Optimism	Order
Planful	Prevention	Reconfiguration	Resolver
Strategic Awareness	Time Optimiser		

Table 2: CAPP®, www.cappeu.com

This assessment, developed by Alex Linley, Janet Willars and Robert Biswas-Diener, gathers three perspectives on strengths:

1. What you do well – Performance
2. What you feel good doing – Energy
3. What you do a lot – Use

From these three perspectives – Energy, Performance and Use – the summary report is able to provide four differentiated strength areas:

- **Realized Strengths** – Strengths that you use frequently with pleasure and which energize you when you use them. It is a sense that *"This is what I was born to do"*.
  o These are the strengths that you *Marshal* in order to use them more and more.

- **Learned Behaviors** – Strengths where you have a high level of performance, but from which you do not derive pleasure and/ or energy. These are capabilities you find either de-energizing or draining and which you might not put to frequent use.
  o These are strengths you need to *Moderate,* use only as appropriate and when needed.

- **Weaknesses** – Things that you perform poorly when you are doing them and that do not enjoy doing, therefore leading to feelings of negativity, demotivation and disengagement. As a result, use may be variable.
  o These are strengths that you need to *Minimize* in their use

- **Unrealized Strengths** – Strengths that you enjoy using, do well and derive pleasure and energy from them, but that you use only infrequently.
  o These are strengths you want *Maximize*, increasing your opportunity to leverage them more frequently.

The comprehensive profile of your strengths in the Realise2 report provides an interaction with a dynamic model, called the Four M model – Marshall, Moderate, Minimize, Maximize.

CAPP® finds that strengths are not fixed, since the context, focus and goals of the work might change. For example, if the demand for a certain *Realised Strength* is not required for success in a current role, it may move into an *Unrealised Strength*. Also, a *Realised Strength* might slip into a *Learned Behavior* because of overuse to the point that it becomes draining. If a role demands the use of a *Weakness*, a strategy is formulated to minimize its use, for example by redefining the role, or finding another person who has that *Weakness* as a *Realized Strength* to fulfill the needed capability.

Using the Realise2® 4M Model, you are able to identify the full portfolio of strengths at a given moment in time and you can consider what the report means to you in practice.

CAPP®, the provider of the Realise2 assessment, uses this methodology for recruitment and teambuilding, in addition to individual development and as a basis for coaching. The clients who have integrated this strengths-based approach into their organizations include Unilever, Thomson Reuters, GlaxoSmithKline, EY, Boehringer Ingelheim, Avery Dennison, and Cisco.

Values in Action

The field of psychology has traditionally focused on mental illness, especially once the *Diagnostic and Statistical Manual of Mental Disorders* (DSM) was developed to categorize mental disorders and ailments. As we find in Chapter 2: Pursuing Optimism and Positivity, Martin Seligman, a traditionally trained psychologist, was determined to focus not on mental illness but on what contributes most to mental well-being and happiness. Thereby, he became one of the fathers of modern positive psychology as a field of study, research, and practice.

Through an exhaustive process, Seligman and psychologist Christopher Peterson created the *Character Strengths and Virtues Handbook*, which is similar to the DSM. The aim was to create a shared language of mental well-being and alignment among professionals in this new field. The research on psychological strengths that shaped the handbook identified six core virtues and 24 character strengths:[49]

---

[49] Peterson, C., & Park, N. (2009). Classifying and measuring strengths of character. In S. J. Lopez & C. R. Snyder (Eds.), *Oxford handbook of positive psychology*, 2nd edition (pp. 25-33). New York: Oxford University Press. Peterson, C., & Seligman, M. E. P. (2004). *Character strengths and virtues: A handbook and classification*. New York: Oxford University Press and Washington, DC: American Psychological Association.

CORE VIRTUES	CHARACTER STRENGTHS
WISDOM AND KNOWLEDGE	• **CREATIVITY:** Originality; adaptive; ingenuity • **CURIOSITY:** Interest; novelty-seeking; exploration; openness to experience • **JUDGMENT:** Critical thinking; thinking things through; open-minded • **LOVE OF LEARNING:** Mastering new skills & topics; systematically adding to knowledge • **PERSPECTIVE:** Wisdom; providing wise counsel; taking the big picture view
COURAGE	• **BRAVERY:** Valor; not shrinking from fear; speaking up for what's right • **PERSEVERANCE:** Persistence; industry; finishing what one starts • **HONESTY:** Authenticity; integrity • **ZEST:** Vitality; enthusiasm; vigor; energy; feeling alive and activated
HUMANITY	• **LOVE:** Both loving and being loved; valuing close relations with others • **KINDNESS:** Generosity; nurturance; care; compassion; altruism; 'niceness' • **SOCIAL INTELLIGENCE:** Emotional intelligence; aware of the motives/feelings of self/others, knowing what makes other people tick
JUSTICE	• **TEAMWORK:** Citizenship; social responsibility; loyalty • **FAIRNESS:** Just; not letting feelings bias decisions about others • **LEADERSHIP:** Organizing group activities; encouraging a group to get things done
TEMPERANCE	• **FORGIVENESS:** Mercy; accepting others' shortcomings; giving people a second chance • **HUMILITY:** Modesty; letting one's accomplishments speak for themselves • **PRUDENCE:** Careful; cautious; not taking undue risks • **SELF-REGULATION:** Self-control; disciplined; managing impulses & emotions
TRANSCENDENCE	• **APPRECIATION OF BEAUTY & EXCELLENCE:** Awe; wonder; elevation • **GRATITUDE:** Thankful for the good; expressing thanks; feeling blessed • **HOPE:** Optimism, future-mindedness; future orientation • **HUMOR:** Playfulness; bringing smiles to others; lighthearted • **SPIRITUALITY:** Religiousness; faith; purpose; meaning

Source: Values in Action (VIA) Assessment

The related online assessment called *Values in Action (VIA)* generates a report that reflects individual values and character strengths. When people exercise these character strengths in their daily lives, the proven benefits include a sense of excitement, motivation to act in accordance with the strength, energy rather than fatigue when using the strength, and continuous learning as to how to build and leverage the strength even more. Many studies have found that when people leverage their signature character strengths every day, they create a positive psychological climate for themselves and others.

StandOut Leadership Strengths

The most recent contribution to the focus on strengths was launched by Marcus Buckingham, co-developer with Donald Clifton of StrengthsFinder®. Buckingham left Gallup when Clifton died in 2003 and launched his own company. He then spent a decade developing a strengths theory and assessment that focuses on strengths in leadership roles. These roles include*:

LEADERSHIP ROLE	YOUR QUESTION	STRENGTHS AND VALUE TO OTHERS
ADVISOR	*What is the best thing to do?*	Valued for expertise, insight, judgment, practical problem solving and desire for excellence
CONNECTOR	*Whom can I connect?*	Valued for networking, combining diverse expertise and skills on high performance teams
CREATOR	*What do I understand?*	Valued for finding patterns underneath life's complexities, creativity
EQUALIZER	*What is the right thing to do?*	Valued for ethics, restoring interconnected order, holding people accountable
INFLUENCER	*How can I move you to act?*	Valued for seeing the outcome early, momentum, ability to move others to action
PIONEER	*What's new?*	Valued for curiosity about the unfamiliar, tolerance of ambiguity, appetite for the unknown
PROVIDER	*Is everyone okay?*	Valued for knowing others' emotional states, inclusion of all, loyalty and support
STIMULATOR	*How can I raise the energy?*	Valued for positivity, humor, presence, energy and exuberance
TEACHER	*What can he learn from this?*	Valued for focus on the other person and his growth, seeing the possibility in imperfection

*Marcus Buckingham, StandOut: Find your Edge. Win at Work, One Thing Productions, Inc. 2011

The StandOut Assessment identifies the top two roles out of a possible nine and generates a 20-page personal report that provides a detailed definition of these combined leadership roles. The report includes: (1) the perceived value that you offer to others, (2) tips on how to take your performance to the next level, (3) steps to achieve high performance as a leader, manager, sales representative, or client service representative, (4) actions to help you avoid potential pitfalls and barriers, and (5) an overview of the ideal careers for your role type.

Based on theory similar to Clifton and Seligman – that when you build on your strengths, you experience exponential improvement in performance, productivity, and results – Buckingham found that building on strengths in your leadership role type provides a unique competitive advantage at work.

In addition, the StandOut platform has a robust website for leadership and team effectiveness. When all team members complete the StandOut assessment, the results are loaded into individual profiles on the platform. The team can then use the information on role strengths to maximize overall performance.

Other features of this platform are personalized best practices, tips and techniques from leaders who have similar strengths. Activities and exercises to conduct with the team are available to ensure that they are getting the most out of their StandOut results.

When focusing positively on strengths, it is critical to:

- become aware of your strengths profile and the profile of others on your team
- keep building on strengths
- mitigate weaknesses if they get in the way of overall performance
- ensure that any mission-critical gaps in strengths on a team are proactively addressed

Only where love and work are one... Is the deed ever really done.

∞Robert Frost, poet, *Two Tramps in Mud Time*

Resources for Exploration and Learning

Below are selected resources for you to assess and leverage your strengths.

Recommended Books

StrengthsFinder 2.0, Tom Rath, Gallup Press, 2007
- o This book gives a comprehensive description of all 34 strengths, offering ways to understand and leverage your strengths, identify strengths in others, and what to do when working with someone with those strengths to motivate and energize their performance.

In the back of the book is a unique code that gives you access to the StrengthsFinder® *assessment.*

Strengths Based Leadership, Tom Rath, Barry Conchie, Gallup Press, 2008
  ○ Rath and Conchie were able to identify and describe the three key capabilities of the most effective leaders, which they describe in this book. A code in the back of the book gives access to a new leadership version of Gallup's StrengthsFinder® **assessment and offers ways to put your strengths in action as a leader.**

StandOut: Find your Edge. Win at Work, Marcus Buckingham, One Thing Productions, Inc, 2011
  ○ This book describes the nine leadership roles and includes a code that allows you to discover your top two roles as a leader.

Readings, Assessments and Videos

READINGS		
25	*State of the American Workplace 2013* Explore the current state of motivation, engagement and leveraging concepts of strengths at work. http://www.gallup.com/strategicconsulting/163007/state-american-workplace.aspx Tiny URL: **http://tinyurl.com/qjcsmxl**	
26	*Lessons from the Gulf Cooperation Council region on what the best managers do differently* Ehssan Abdallah, Ashish Ahluwalia, Gallup Business Journal, November 2013 http://businessjournal.gallup.com/content/165704/managers-create-high-performance-cultures.aspx Tiny URL: **http://tinyurl.com/l8oeuva**	
ASSESSMENT		
27	Clifton StrengthsFinder® assessment: Discover your 5 Signature Strengths https://www.gallupstrengthscenter.com/?utm_source=externalpostlaunch&utm_medium=email&utm_Recampaign=ESF_GSCAnnouncement Tiny URL: **http://tinyurl.com/l6zrgms**	

28	**Realise2® assessment: contact Capp® to explore certification in the instrument, or its potential use in your organization** http://www.cappeu.com/Contact.aspx Tiny URL: **http://tinyurl.com/m8ts7a2**	
29	Values in Action free assessment: Identify Your Values *http://www.viacharacter.org*	
30	StandOut **assessment: Receive a profile of your two top leadership roles/strengths** https://www.tmbc.com/store/standout-assessment Tiny URL: **http://tinyurl.com/p67gosx**	
VIDEOS	Once you have taken the Gallup StrengthsFinder® assessment there are videos available on each of the 34 strengths you can watch to understand that strength better by going to the Gallup Strengths platform.	

CHAPTER 5

Fostering Engagement and Flow

Purpose and Outcomes

This chapter brings together two important concepts in the development of positive organizations and positive leadership – Engagement and Flow.

The focus is on the responsibility of the organization to foster employee engagement, by providing the context in which workers can experience *flow*, because they:

- know their work is valued
- understand that their work is an important contribution to the success of the enterprise
- enjoy their work because they are doing what they love every day
- achieve high performance and productivity because they are fully engaged

In 2001, Campbell's Soup, Inc., was seeing its demise as a leading brand. A precipitous decline in sales and intensifying competition had led to rumors that the company was a takeover target. At this time, in an attempt to stop the downward spiral and salvage the company, Douglas Conant was tapped to leave Nabisco to become the new CEO at Campbell's. Conant's agenda was to bring the struggling company up to 'extraordinary' performance. No small ambition!

Among more routine actions, such as cost control, a more sophisticated marketing strategy and innovations in the product line, Conant focused on engaging the workforce.

To win in the marketplace, we believe you must first win in the workplace. I'm obsessed with keeping employee engagement front and center and keeping up energy around it.
∞Douglas Conant, CEO Campbell's Soup, Inc.

Conant worked with Campbell's to create a vision that resonated, "*Campbell valuing people, people valuing Campbell*". In addition, he worked with direct line managers to support them in their efforts to engage employees. Conant also began to use every opportunity to demonstrate that this vision was a reality, for example, he sends about 20 thank you notes a day to employees at all levels.

The total return on Campbell stock gained more than 30 percent since 2001, during which time Standard & Poor's 500 Index lost more than 10 percent. Campbell's dynamic success in this effort proves again that employee engagement correlates very closely to shareholder returns.

Today, the employee engagement focus at Campbell's continues to evolve. A main target and objective at Campbell's currently is to achieve 100 percent employee engagement in CSR (Corporate Social Responsibility) and sustainability by 2020. This emphasis gives employees an opportunity to understand and support a higher purpose and meaning in their work. Already, key initiatives have reduced water consumption by 264 million gallons, cut 280,000 tons of greenhouse gas emissions, and built a 59 acre 10 mega-watt solar field.

Campbell's finds that this effort is contributing significantly to the attraction and retention of the most talented workers, especially millennials, who want to know the values and culture of the organization supports their own values, because the millennials strongly desire to contribute positively to their community, society and the world.

Engagement and Flow as Positive Forces in Change

There are only three measurements that tell you nearly everything you need to know about your organization's overall performance: employee engagement, customer satisfaction, and cash flow...It goes without saying that no company, small or large, can win over the long run without energized employees who believe in the mission and understand how to achieve it.
∞Jack Welch, former CEO of GE

Today's global economy has brought us fast-paced, increasingly complex changes unlike any we have ever experienced. The disruptive and discontinuous changes in business, regulatory, technological, and international trends have compelled organizations to change their business models, either through a merger & acquisition, a restructuring, or a strategy transformation.

Since these types of changes are driven from the top of the organization, the only way to ensure continued employee engagement is to carefully manage transitions from the current to the future state. Otherwise, disengagement and the loss of key talent are inevitable, as employees are likely in times of major change to fear a loss of status, control, and confidence, all of which leads to resistance.

While every change initiative is unique with its own special challenges, the keys to driving employee engagement during change include:

- visibility of the leadership in a two-way communication with employees
- engagement of the employees in decision-making, especially in their area of responsibility
- employee awareness of career opportunities and pathways in the new framework
- development of employee skills that are necessary for their future success
- a sense of community and connection between leaders and co-workers

It is well-known, people join companies, but they leave their bosses. It's especially important to select and train managers who are able to develop people and provide tasks that create flow – leveraging strengths and providing a sense of meaning and purpose. If people are given the opportunity to experience a strong connection to their work and are able to apply their talent, skills, and knowledge – both utilizing existing capabilities while mastering new ones – they will be fully engaged and willing to give their commitment and discretionary efforts to achieve success.

What is Engagement?

Engagement is the alignment of the individual with the mission, vision and values of the organization, an emotional and intellectual commitment to the organization, and a willingness to provide discretionary effort to achieve the best results.

Employee engagement sets the stage for each employee to go beyond the specifics of his or her job description and achieve a state of *flow* or optimal experience. This is achieved by:

- staying fully aware and in the moment
- finding challenges and opportunities that stretch and develop desired skills
- enhancing his or her contribution to the team and the organization as a whole

Engagement reduces stress, depression, turnover, absenteeism, dissatisfaction and cynicism, while at the same time increasing commitment, effort, empowerment, happiness, satisfaction and a sense of fulfillment.[50]

Why Does Engagement Matter?

An engaged workforce has many significant benefits. Kenexa research found in 2009 that the most engaged companies have five times the total shareholder return.[51] Towers Perrin found that companies with engagement cultures have a 6 percent higher net profit margin.[52] Gallup research in 2013 found that work units in the top 25 percent engagement rankings have *"significantly higher productivity, profitability, less turnover and absenteeism, and fewer safety incidents than those in the bottom 25 percent."*[53] The Bureau of National Affairs estimates that U.S. businesses

---

[50] G. Chen, *Subject-object meaningfulness in knowledge work.* Honors Thesis. University of Michigan.
[51] The Impact of Employee Engagement, Kenexa® Research Institute, 2009.
[52] Global Workforce Study, Towers Perrin, 2011.
[53] State of the American Workplace, Gallup, 2013.

lose $11 billion annually due to employee turnover, while many studies find that companies with engaged employees have higher retention rates, thereby decreasing recruiting and hiring costs.

Employee disengagement is at an all-time high, and Gallup estimates that *active disengagement* costs the U.S. approximately $450 to $550 billion per year. A Swedish WOLF study into the cost of disengagement found that those dissatisfied with their jobs are more likely to be hospitalized or die from a heart attack, increasing healthcare costs for the organization.[54]

Gallup also discovered that of the 100 million workers in the U.S., 20 percent are actively disengaged, and 50 percent are not engaged. Thus 70 percent of workers fall in the neutral to actively disengaged range. These employees have *quit and stayed* – a cost without value. The impact of direct line managers on performance is measured as well by the Q12, 12 simple statements that can assess employ engagement. Using the Q 12 Gallup found three categories of employees. In a random sample of 1,003 workers in the US who assessed whether their managers focused on their strengths and positive characteristics, or their weaknesses and deficiencies:

1. Of those whose managers **ignored** them, 40 percent were *actively disengaged*. It brings to mind the joke about a visitor to a large business who asked *"How many people work here?"* and the answer was *"Half of them!"*

2. Managers who focused on employees' **weaknesses** cut this *active disengagement* to 22 percent.

3. For workers who believed their managers focused on their **talents and strengths**, however, the level of *active disengagement* fell to 1 percent. And almost 61 percent of these workers were fully engaged, which in 2013 is more than twice the average of overall US workers.[55]

---

[54] Managerial leadership and ischaemic heart disease among employees: *the Swedish WOLF study.* Nyberg A, Alfredsson L, Theorell T, Westerlund H, Vahtera J, Kivimäki M. Occup Environ Med, 2009.

[55] *State of the American Workplace,* Gallup, Inc., 2013,pp 47-51.

HIGHLY ENGAGED	An emotional and intellectual connection to the mission, vision, and goals of the organization, and a commitment to provide discretionary energy and skills to achieve the highest results.
MODERATELY ENGAGED	A positive view of the organization and the leadership, but not fully invested in the future, nor willing to commit extra initiative and efforts to the overall goals.
NEUTRAL	A commitment to show up at work and go through the motions, but without enthusiasm or positive connection.
SOMEWHAT DISENGAGED	Shows up at work without emotional commitment to being productive and already looking for opportunities elsewhere or maybe running an eBay business on-the-job.
ACTIVELY DISENGAGED	Workers who sabotage their jobs and employers, spreading discontent and dissatisfaction that mirrors their own emotional state. Their negative energy is contagious.

The organization is responsible for setting the culture, context and framework for full engagement, and this obligation cannot be ignored. The drivers of a culture of engagement for the individual include:

- provision of challenging work
- variety on the job
- use and development of different skills
- personal discretion as to how to achieve objectives
- frequent feedback – 80 percent positive and strengths-based to 20 percent developmental[56]
- opportunity to make important contributions

When people feel that they are pursuing a deep and meaningful purpose and are engaged in work that is personally relevant, there is a positive impact on health, turnover, and absenteeism. Engagement also increases commitment, happiness, and satisfaction.[57]

What is Flow?

According to Mihaly Csikszentmihalyi, a co-founder of the emerging field of positive psychology, the concept of *flow* is a state of mindful, energized focus on an enjoyable activity that is so absorbing that external realities, such as the passing of time and physical discomfort, don't seem to matter. The experience of flow is characterized by five components:

---

[56] Stephen R. Covey, *The 7 Habits of Highly Effective People*, 1989 & 2004, Simon & Schuster.
[57] Chen, G., Subject-object meaningfulness in knowledge work, Honors thesis, University of Michigan 2000.

1. focused concentration in the present moment
2. opportunities to take action
3. freedom to express creativity
4. development of new skills
5. becoming lost in the interaction

> *Enjoyment appears at the boundary between boredom and anxiety, when the challenges are just balanced with the person's capacity to act.*
>
> ∞ Mihaly Csikszentmihalyi, author, researcher and co-founder of field of positive psychology

Flow produces an *optimal experience,* where the body or mind is stretched to its limits in a voluntary effort to accomplish a difficult and worthwhile goal.[58] In this state, the emotions are mastered into a positive, energized alignment with the task at hand.

This experience combines a specific challenge with the individual's skills. At any point along the continuum of flow, these two are well-matched. If the skill exceeds the challenge, boredom results. If the challenge too far exceeds the skill, employees can end up feeling anxiety or panic.

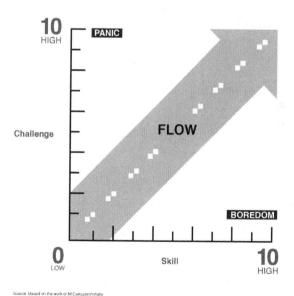

Source: Based on the work of M.Csikszentmihalyi

---

[58] Mihaly Csikszentmihalyi, *Flow: The Psychology of Optimal Experience,* Harper Perennial, 1990.

It is recommended that in daily life and on the job, the balance among these three be:

- 20 percent spent in the upper left area of achieving stretch goals
- 65-70 percent spent in *Flow*
- 5-15 percent in the lower right area where doing something costs you very little in energy and focus.

Csikszentmihalyi encourages organizations to create interventions to enhance and support flow in the workplace and identifies three conditions that must be present to create flow experiences:

1. sufficient balance between the task and the challenge
2. clear goals, especially in terms of where the task fits into the overall organizational plan and success – creating a sense of meaning and purpose
3. immediate and frequent feedback to increase motivation and keep results on target

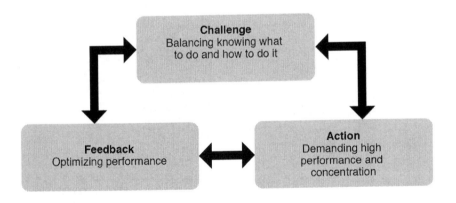

Building Engagement and Flow in the Workplace

For the individual, there is also a *personal* responsibility to derive meaning from work by (1) looking beyond the boundaries of the position description, (2) thinking creatively about what additional value he/she could provide, and (3) not staying fixed on one method but instead, discovering new options. Flow that is produced in optimal work experiences, such as in a career or primarily in a *calling*, creates positive energy and a sense of discovery. It supports growth to an ever higher level of performance.

MEANING OF WORK	MOTIVATION	OBJECTIVE
A JOB	Financial and material rewards	Obtain financial resources to engage in another activity, e.g. "I want to purchase a new car."
A CAREER	Success	Achieve personal growth, recognition, and capability development, e.g. "I want to publish a book."
A CALLING	The work itself	Work for a greater good beyond personal benefit or reward, e.g. "I care deeply about what I am doing."

Although organizations have a great responsibility to provide the context for meaning, there is much an **individual** can do to increase both engagement and flow in work experiences by creating a calling for themselves. Martin Seligman tells a story of an orderly in a hospital where he was visiting a friend in a coma. As he sat there, the orderly came into the room, removed the bed pan, cleaned the floor and then began to adjust and replace the framed pictures on the wall, occasionally stepping back to see whether the selected picture created the atmosphere he was trying to produce.

When Seligman asked him about his activities, the orderly answered: *"I'm responsible for the health of all these patients. Take Mr. Miller here. He hasn't woken up since they brought him in, but when he does, I want to make sure he sees beautiful things right away."*[59] This orderly had developed a higher meaning and purpose for his work on his own, giving careful consideration to what might be the most inspiring picture for the patient.

People typically associate one of three kinds of meaning to their work: a job, a career, or a calling. Obviously, this orderly found a *calling* in his work.

However for full engagement, the **organization** must create the situations and opportunities for people to achieve flow on-the-job. It has been found in multiple research studies that people stay primarily with employment that matches their deeply embedded life interests. This has led to the notion of *Job Sculpting*[60], which is the art of creating customized

---

[59] Martin Seligman, *Authentic Happiness*, Free Press, 2002, pp.167-168.
[60] *Job sculpting: The art of retaining your best people*, Timothy Butler and James Waldroop, Harvard Business School Working Knowledge, 12/21/1999.

career paths that resonate with individuals by enabling them to pursue doing work they love – in other words – engaging in flow experiences.

Because many are actually hazy about their values and strengths, it is important to assist them in this process of self-discovery. Instruments helpful in building this insight are StengthsFinder®, Realise2® and Values in Action. (See Chapter 5: Leveraging Strengths)

In addition, the creators of the job-sculpting concept Timothy Butler and James Waldroop, have identified eight life interests that can be used as a key tool for employees to discover their inherent interests. The Business Career Interest Inventory (BCII) is founded on their belief that careers should be based on interests not skills.

The BCII provides a measure of interest patterns as they apply to business work roles and work environments in the following core function areas:

APPLICATION OF TECHNOLOGY	QUANTITATIVE ANALYSIS	THEORY DEVELOPMENT AND CONCEPTUAL THINKING	CREATIVE PRODUCTION
Interested in learning about and using new technologies. Enjoys analyzing and designing (or redesigning) business processes such as production and operations systems.	Prefers solving business issues by "running the numbers." Enjoys building computer models, doing financial and market research analysis.	Interested in high-level abstract thinking about business issues, and the theory (as well as the practice) of business strategy. Enjoys doing in-depth research.	Enjoys brainstorming novel ideas for products and services. Prefers early, creative stages of businesses and projects to later "maintenance" phase.

COUNSELING AND MENTORING	MANAGING PEOPLE AND TEAMS	ENTERPRISE CONTROL	INFLUENCE THROUGH LANGUAGE AND IDEAS
Enjoys developing employees and others to reach their fullest potential. Often prefers work with high social values, and organizations with a collaborative culture.	Interested working with and through others on a day-to-day basis to accomplish concrete business goals. Enjoys leading teams, and prefers line management to staff roles.	Interested in setting business strategy and having the power to ensure that the strategy is carried out. Ultimately wants general management role.	Enjoys persuading others, whether to buy a product or service, or to support a proposal. Often enjoys making presentations, but may prefer writing or one-to-one negotiations.

Source: www.CareerLadder.com

Once you are aware of the portfolio of values, strengths and interests of your employee, a coaching discussion to explore how to leverage and integrate these on-the-job will begin a job-sculpting career approach and result in high employee engagement and increased flow experiences at work. (See Chapter 9: Coaching for Positive Change)

Promoting the feeling of being valued and involved is the strongest driver of employee engagement. Since the research has shown that employee engagement highly correlates with positive business outcomes, organizations that embrace the drivers of engagement, intentionally creating a high performance culture, provide the context for individuals to achieve their highest potential.

Appreciate everything your associates do for the business. Nothing else can quite substitute for a few well-chosen, well-timed, sincere words of praise. They're absolutely free and worth a fortune.

∞Sam Walton, founder of Walmart

Resources for Exploration and Learning

The resources below will help you to build your understanding and appreciation of *Engagement* at work and how to create work that offers the pleasure and enjoyment of *Flow*.

Recommended Books

Employee Engagement 2.0: How to Motivate Your Team for High Performance, (A Real-World Guide for Busy Managers), The Kruse Group, 2012

- A quick read and a simple action plan to foster employee engagement.

Flow: The Psychology of Optimal Experience, M. Csikszentmihalyi, Harper Perennial, 1990

- Flow is used to describe a state of mind characterized by deep enjoyment, creativity and total involvement. This "optimal experience" is can be achieved by intentionally allowing the positive to enter our mind.

Articles, Assessment & Video

ARTICLES		
31	Job Sculpting: The Art of Retaining Your Best People, Timothy Butler and James Waldroop, Working Knowledge, Harvard Business School, 1999 http://hbswk.hbs.edu/archive/875.html Tiny URL: **http://tinyurl.com/lbxrcel**	
32	*Why Employee Engagement: These 28 Research Studies Prove the Benefits*, Kevin Kruse, Forbes,09/04/12 http://www.forbes.com/sites/kevinkruse/2012/09/04/why-employee-engagement/3/ Tiny URL: **http://tinyurl.com/azz54qs**	
33	*How to Tackle U.S. Employees' Stagnating Engagement*, Gallup Business Journal, 06/11/13 http://businessjournal.gallup.com/content/162953/tackle-employees-stagnating-engagement.aspx Tiny URL: **http://tinyurl.com/kefs7dv**	
ASSESSMENTS		
34	**The Business Career Interest Inventory (BCCI)** Assessment and Report http://www.careerdiscovery.com/hbspsba/bcii_start.html Tiny URL: **http://tinyurl.com/p5mz2bn**	
35	**Integrating Assessment Themes using Business Career Interest Inventory** (BCCI) Process to understand and leverage your BCCI results http://www.skillscan.com/sites/default/files/BCII percent20Integration percent20Client percent20Form percent20Final.pdf Tiny URL: **http://tinyurl.com/o22a37q**	
VIDEO		
36	**Flow, the Secret to Happiness**, TED talk, February 2004. Mihaly Csikszentmihalyi on flow http://www.ted.com/talks/mihaly_csikszentmihalyi_on_flow.html Tiny URL: **http://tinyurl.com/lhdzo4**	

CHAPTER 7

Building Trust

Purpose and Outcomes

This chapter outlines the crucial contribution that trust makes to the success of relationships, organizations, economies, governments, and businesses.

The content will enable you to:

- learn and apply the *trust equation*
- examine the high cost of low trust environments
- build trusted advisor relationships on teams, with clients and in organizations
- leverage trust to overcome resistance and achieve success in leading change

---

One of the many silver cart street vendors in New York noticed that the line for customers who wanted coffee and doughnuts was growing ever longer. Some potential customers became so impatient, they just stopped waiting and left. In order to speed up the line, the vendor decided to let the customers use an honor system and make their own change. His was probably one of the first businesses to have that level of trust in their customers!

The result – a much faster line, more satisfied customers, and an actual increase in income, because of the speed which enabled more customers to quickly get their coffee and a donut, and because if the cost for the item was $1.75, the person in a hurry generally put $2.00 in the container and didn't bother to take the $.25 change! Completely supporting the knowledge that trust increases speed and reduces cost!

> *Trust is the glue of life. It's the most essential ingredient in effective communication. It's the foundational principle that holds all relationships.*
>
> ∞ Stephen R. Covey, American business author

Trust as a Positive Force in Change

In *The World is Flat*, Thomas Friedman describes the new economic context in which globalization and technology are causing ever more rapid changes in society.[61] The new interdependence Friedman portrays demands that people must build relationships across traditional boundaries and barriers, in many cases destroying the former limits. This *flat world* requires rapid, agile responsiveness and change. Without trust, however, it's impossible to implement successful change, especially change of this magnitude.

It is well worth the effort to build a culture of trust. Trust in an organization is the social capital that enables it to thrive in uncertainty and ambiguity, and it can be a very valuable intangible asset. Social capital promotes cooperation, commitment, extra effort, continuous improvement, and information exchange. All of which can all help an organization survive and achieve a competitive advantage.

Nevertheless, the change being promoted is often accompanied by poor communication, increased conflict, broken promises, and a lack of honesty. Individuals who are not supported through change by a climate of trust respond in 'survival' mode to the high levels of uncertainty. In turn, this survival mentality creates a culture of hidden agendas, negative competition, politics, secrecy, and excessive rules and regulations to control behavior. Employees end up feeling powerless, out of control, and helpless. These unhealthy behaviors and negative emotions further erode employee commitment, satisfaction, and engagement. The end result is that employees resist the change, and it fails.

The Value of Trust

Organizations that proactively create a culture of high trust – even in the midst of change – build employee, consumer, and investor confidence.

---

[61] Thomas Friedman, *The World is Flat*, Picador, 2007.

During times of uncertainty and change, organizational actions and policies that promote a culture of trust include:

- investing in employees
- communicating openly and honestly
- behaving in an ethical and socially responsible manner
- providing a measure of job security

A Merger with Trust

The merger of a formerly independent function into the parent company threatened to create redundancies and potential layoffs. However, the leader of the independent group chose to maintain positivity and build trust. In order to sustain employee engagement, confidence, and energy, he viewed the changing circumstances with an open mind rather than judgment, modeling the way for the staff to remain positive and optimistic.

Every Friday afternoon, he gathered the team and gave an honest update on what was happening, thereby establishing an atmosphere of trustworthiness, reliability, and credibility. He helped everyone to make sense of what was changing, he openly and transparently shared information, and he listened carefully to their concerns.

As a result, his team continued to produce excellent work, and during the merger they earned a reputation with the parent company as the best employees. No one on his team was laid off.

The only way to achieve success in this VUCA world (see Chapter 3: Practicing Mindfulness, page 35) is to focus on building, enhancing, and practicing the behaviors and attitudes that create trust – integrity, reliability, caring, fairness, competence, and loyalty. As we find in the story about leading transformational change at Campbell's Soup in Chapter 6: Fostering Engagement and Flow, when leaders and managers act in harmony with the behaviors and attitudes of trust in mind, employees become more creative and empowered, share information, collaborate, are willing to take risks, and show less resistance to the change. High trust reduces costs, accelerates productivity, and encourages high performance in the midst of change.

What is Trust?

The concept of trust is complex, broad, and elusive. In fact, there is little agreement on a conclusive definition of trust, as it is contextually driven and is subject to many interconnecting aspects, including cultural variations.

Simply stated, trust is a result of a positive relationship between two parties. It's found in a situation where each party has an expectation that the other party will not harm him/her at a time when he/she is vulnerable.

Trust has both logical and emotional components. Trust develops over time in a relationship, as information is shared, personal concerns are revealed, and favors are given. Trust increases when no injury comes from the vulnerability, i.e. confidences are not betrayed, the information shared is reliable, and favors are returned. The credibility, reliability, and honesty of the other person are proven over time, and this historical data is then used to calculate whether a person is trustworthy.

The Study of Trust

Those involved in the field of research on the impact of trust have very similar descriptions of the five major categories of actions and behaviors that we assess and upon which we base our trust, whether individual or organizational:

- *Capability/Competence/Credibility* = The skills and ability to deliver on commitments
- *Reliability/Dependability/Predictability* = Production of the expected results, every time/on time
- *Intimacy/Empathy/Benevolence* = Placing the interests of an individual, group, and/or company first
- *Sincerity/Honesty/Transparency* = Holding no hidden agendas, actions align with words
- *Ethics/Integrity/Trustworthiness* = Adhering to principles, values, and character

The willingness to trust another party is based on the history of a relationship that inspires positive expectations, coupled by the propensity of humans to trust. This propensity to trust begins during the first two years of life, when the growth of basic trust is the first state of psychosocial development.[62] When an infant finds that his/her caregivers are reliable and dependable, the infant develops feelings of security, trust, and optimism. (See Chapter 2: Pursuing Optimism and Positivity)

The best way to learn if you can trust somebody is to trust them.
∞ Ernest Hemingway, American author

Neuroscience has revealed that there is a correlation between the exercise of trust and the production of oxytocin, called the *trust* or *love* hormone.[63] When trust is shared, it is a strong predictor of subjective well-being because it enhances positive emotions and interpersonal relationships. However, if the infant's caregivers fail to provide a loving and safe environment, this can lead to later feelings of frustration, suspicion, and withdrawal, harming the propensity to trust.

Trust always implies some degree of risk. Although we have a positive expectation, trust implies that the person might not do what is expected. We are entrusting them with something of value to us, hoping that they will do no harm. This sense of risk puts us in the *"I hope he will do it"* range when we trust another person.

Thus, trust is a calculated risk – a leap of emotional commitment based on data, but a risk nonetheless. And because there is a risk involved, practically everyone has experienced a betrayal of trust. Behavior that harms another person brings forth highly negative emotions, and the resulting distrust leads to resistance, withdrawal, and separation.

Trust but verify.
∞ Ronald Reagan, 40th President of the United States

---

[62] Wikipedia Online Encyclopedia.
[63] M. Kosfeld, M. Heinrichs, P. Zak, U Fischbacher, E. Fehr, *Oxytocin increases trust in humans*, nature vol. 435, June 2005.

The *cost of low trust* is great in relationships – whether it is between two people, among a group of people, or within an entire organization – but the *value of high trust* is even greater.

The High Costs of Low Trust

There is no dispute that trust is critical to high performance in humans and organizations. The Watson Wyatt WorkUSA Survey in 2002 of almost 13,000 workers found that high trust organizations had a 286 percent greater total return to their shareholders compared with low trust organizations of the same size and industry.[64]

According to the Great Place to Work Institute, trust is the primary defining characteristic of at least 60 percent of the criteria used to select the Fortune 100 Best Companies to Work for.[65] Amy Lyman, co-founder of The Great Place to Work Institute, has studied trust in organizations for the past two decades. She has found that three characteristics of trust surface in all of her research: credibility, respect, and fair treatment.

Unfortunately, in the twenty-first century, trust is on a steep decline in all sectors of human endeavor. Many recent polls paint an alarming picture:

- an Associated Press poll found that only 33 percent of Americans believe those they encounter in their everyday activities can be trusted.[66]
- the 2012 Edelman Trust Barometer shows that the number of *distrusting* countries was growing rapidly.[67]
- four Gallup polls on trust all indicate a precipitous drop in Americans' trust of government, the church/organized religion, news media, and banks.[68]

> *Trust is like the air we breathe. When it is present, nobody notices. But when it's absent, everyone notices.*
> ∞Warren Buffet, investor and philanthropist

---

[64] Linda Bower, *Employee Commitment Directly Affects Company's Bottom Line*, 2001.
[65] *Assess Your Organization*, GreatPlacetoWork Institute®.
[66] AP-GfK poll, October 2013.
[67] 2012 Edelman Trust Barometer.
[68] Trust in Government, Gallup Poll; U.S. Confidence in Organized Religion at Low Point, Gallup Poll; Americans' Confidence in Newspapers Continues to Erode, Gallup Poll; Americans' Confidence in Banks Falls to Record Low, Gallup Poll.

In a 2010 *Forbes* article, *The Economics of Trust*, Tim Harford describes a low trust scenario: You go to the convenience store to purchase milk, but the refrigerator is locked. In order to get the milk you want, you and the shopkeeper must negotiate how to exchange your money for the milk, whether you're going to hand the money over first, or whether he is going to hand over the milk first. Finally, you manage to arrange an elaborate simultaneous exchange. Consider how difficult a more complicated transaction would be in such a low trust context, such as getting a mortgage or conducting an eBay transaction.[69]

The trend toward low trust is a critical social and business issue. Distrust is expensive since it requires additional legal review and stipulation of contracts, regulation, and bureaucratic oversight. For example, after fraud brought down Enron, Tyco, and WorldCom, the Sarbanes-Oxley (SOX) Act was passed in the United States to help restore public confidence and strengthen corporate governance.

However, the time and money needed to comply with the regulations is very costly. According to a survey of public companies by Financial Executives International (FEI) in January 2004, audit fees due to SOX were expected to increase approximately 38 percent during the first year of compliance with section 404. According to another more recent study, the net aggregate private cost of Sarbanes-Oxley compliance amounts to $1.4 trillion.[70]

The dramatic economic cost of low trust is described in Covey's *High Cost of Low Trust* calculation on YouTube.[71] 96 percent of **engaged** employees said they trust the people who run their companies' finances, while only 68 percent of **actively disengaged** employees agreed.[72] (See Chapter 6: Fostering Engagement and Flow, pages 78–80)

This **trust deficit** impacts all of us (1) in the cost of processes and procedures put into place to ensure control; (2) in wastes of time, talent, energy, engagement, and turnover; and (3) in the continuing cost of fraud.

On the other hand, Stephen M.R. Covey finds that there is a **trust**

---

[69] The Economics of Trust, Tim Harford, *Forbes*, July 2010.

[70] Ivy Xiying Zhang, *Economic Consequences of the Sarbanes-Oxley Act of 2002*, Ph.D. dissertation, William E. Simon Graduate School of Business Administration, University of Rochester, February 2005.

[71] *The High Cost of Low Trust*, Franklin Covey, YouTube video, December 2010.

[72] *Warning: Corporate Scandals May Demoralize Employees*, Gallup Business Journal, 2002.

dividend in high trust organizations. He calls trust a performance multiplier in that it *"accelerates growth, enhances innovation, improves collaboration, strengthens partnering, speeds up execution, and heightens loyalty."*[73]

How Can You Build Trust?

To succeed, leaders must build trust during times of change and ambiguity. Leaders who have first established and continue to maintain trust find that even in uncertain situations, their constituents will align with them. These workers will engage and exceed expectations for a leader they trust. But with a leader who is not trusted, there will be resistance, disengagement, and low productivity. The workers will do only just enough to avoid getting fired.

Furthermore, leaders who trust their subordinates are more likely to delegate tasks to them, expressing confidence that they can do it. And even though there is a risk, employee mistakes will be seen as learning opportunities, not threats to their careers.

To become a trustworthy leader and a trusted advisor, there are two simple rules.

Simple rule #1: *Begin with yourself.*

In the seminal book, *The Trusted Advisor*[74] David Maister, Charles Green, and Robert Galford the four components of trustworthiness are described in a *trust equation*. As you review the elements, you can measure your personal attitudes and behaviors in establishing trustworthiness:

---

[73] Stephen R.M. Covey, *The Speed of Trust: The One Thing That Changes Everything,* Free Press, 2006, pp.114 – 115.
[74] David Maister, Charles Green, and Robert Galford, *The Trusted Advisor,* Touchstone, 2001, pp. 69-85.

Trustworthiness

=

Credibility + Reliability + Intimacy

Self Orientation

Source: Daniel Maister, Charles Green: The Trusted Advisor, Simon & Schuster 2001

The result of the calculations on the Trust Equation must be >1. If Self-Orientation is high, you will not be trusted – regardless of how well you do the top line in terms of credibility, reliability, and intimacy.

The components are defined as follows"

CREDIBILITY	Content expertise and presence; honest about limitations	Do you spend the time necessary every day to build and maintain your cutting-edge expertise?
RELIABILITY	Dependable; consistent behaviors	Do you do what you say you will do and inform all stakeholders if you are not able to meet the target?
INTIMACY	Caring and putting the interests of others and the business first	Are you compassionate and careful to listen to the concerns, interests, and goals of others?
SELF-ORIENTATION	Putting your own agenda first	Do you promote yourself and your goals ahead of others?

Your reputation and integrity are everything. Follow through on what you say you're going to do. Your credibility can only be built over time, and it is built from the history of your words and actions.

∞Maria Razumich-Zec, Regional Vice President, USA East Coast, The Peninsula Hotels and General Manager, The Peninsula Chicago

---

HubSpot Places Trust in Employees

Brian Halligan and Dharmesh Shah, the leadership at HubSpot, have followed a visible and encompassing strategy to create a culture of trust. Founded at the Massachusetts Institute of Technology in June 2006, HubSpot focused on *inbound marketing* – drawing customers to a client's website through the promotion of blogs, podcasts, videos, eBooks, search engine optimization, interesting website content, and social media.

The leaders realized, however, that the new organizational paradigm required a new employer/employee contract. They eliminated all traditional human resources policies and procedures regarding social media, travel, sick days, working from home, and replaced these with one simple rule: *Use. Good. Judgment.*[75]

Doing this, they decided to promote the motivation of their employees by trusting them to do the right thing.

Simple Rule #2: Create a *culture of trust.*

Begin with integrity, values, and character. Principled leaders weave values into every message, communication, behavior, and action and do not expect others to behave in ways that these leaders are unwilling to model themselves.

- *What are your values, and do you live and breathe them every day? Are your values aligned with the organization's values? What do you do to take the initiative to be an ethical corporate citizen?*

Share information with openness and transparency. Engage in a continuous dialogue with colleagues and all stakeholder groups about strategies, goals, and commitments. Ensure that all can see themselves in that future vision, and keep your promises. Be authentic in your communication; nothing destroys trust like dishonesty.

---

[75] Dharmesh Shah determined to focus on building a culture of trust at HubSpot and spent many hours in conversations and discussions with employees to refine this so that it might become a 21st century Culture Code for like-minded organizations. http://www.slideshare.net/HubSpot/the-hubspot-culture-code-creating-a-company-we-love. (Tiny URL: http://tinyurl.com/cv3nv5u)

- *What is your communication strategy? Are you authentic and honest even when you believe the message might be uncomfortable for others? How do you use storytelling, anecdotes, and images to inspire the imaginations of others?*

Treat others with appreciation and respect. Empower others to do their work, respecting diversity and giving recognition where earned. Encourage others to leverage their strengths, rather than try to fix their weaknesses. Involve the entire organization in creating solutions. Invest in employee learning and growth.

- *How do you engage others to align with you? How do you express gratitude when your employees go above and beyond in accomplishing important things, whether large or small? What is your strategy for getting everyone to play to their strengths?*

Be genuinely interested in others, and put their interests ahead of your own. Exhibit empathy and sensitivity to the needs of others, and encourage them to do the same. Trust grows out of the belief that you understand and can relate to their circumstances. Connect emotionally, and try to comprehend the perspectives, interests, and goals of others.

- *When in a conversation, how much time do you spend in inquiry, and how much time in advocacy? Do you ask iterative, exploratory questions that go below the surface? Do you listen empathically, even when you disagree?*

Take thoughtful risks to improve service and products for the customer. To foster a culture of innovation and collaboration, demonstrate that risk-taking is encouraged and that if a carefully considered risk goes wrong, the focus is on the learning opportunity, not blame.

- *Do you work hard to innovate and improve services and products for customers even when it involves some degree of risk? How do you encourage innovation and collaboration in your team? How do you guarantee that they focus on delighting the customer?*

Because trust is the engine that drives everything positive, trust is a non-negotiable trait.

The bottom line is to pursue and promote trust and advocate its pursuit in your organization. Examine yourself and the culture in your own place of work. If trust is lacking, take the necessary steps to improve this critical capability. The foundation of trust will permeate every aspect of your company – the people, the products they produce, and the corporate culture.

Resources for Exploration and Learning

To learn more about how to build trust in relationships, below is a selection of online assessments, websites, videos and books.

Recommended Books

The Trusted Leader, Robert Galford, Anne Seibold Drapeau, The Free Press, 2002
  - o   The Trusted Leader deals with building internal, managerial and organizational trust. The different kinds of trust are described along with diagnostic tools to identify if trust is lacking and where trust needs to be built or restored when it has been lost. This is the most comprehensive guide on trust for managers.

The Trusted Advisor, David Maister, Charles Green, Robert Galford, Touchstone, 2001
  - o   The key to building successful business relationships is the ability to earn the trust and confidence of others. The authors demonstrate the relevance and criticality of trust, offer and describe the Trust Equation and tell stories and anecdotes of trust, or lack thereof, in the workplace.

The Speed of Trust, Stephen R.M. Covey, Free Press, 2006
  - o   Trust is described as the engine of the global economy, essential to lower costs and higher speed in every transaction and relationship. Also explained is a method to immediately work on establishing a trust foundation to achieve successful high performance.

The Trust Edge, David Horsager, The Free Press, 20009

o   Based on current research, this book shares the 8 pillars of trust and how to leverage them to improve relationships, reputations, retention, revenue, and results. An environment of trust leads to greater innovation, morale, and productivity. Leaders discover how to build and maintain trust of their leadership, in their brand and among their clients and customers.

The Trustworthy Leader, Amy Lyman, The Great Place to Work Institute, 2012

o   Based on 20 years of intensive research on the value of trust in companies and the undeniable link to profitability and success, this book draws from examples of the Best Companies to Work For. Lyman describes six elements that demonstrate a leader's trustworthiness and how leaders can authentically master and leverage these.

The Great Workplace, Michael Burchel, Jennifer Robin, Josey-Bass, 2011

o   The model employed by the Great Place to Work Institute for the past 30 years to rank companies is explored, identifying the measures and trends of the best places to work. The measures and the value of creating a great workplace have found resonance in 40 countries around the world.

Articles, Assessment, Polls & Videos

ARTICLES		
37	*Trusted Advisor Fieldbook, free e-books* http://trustedadvisor.com/books/the-trusted-advisor-fieldbook Tiny URL: **http://tinyurl.com/ckohmtk**	
38	*AP-GfK poll,* October 2013. Lack of trust in American society http://ap-gfkpoll.com/featured/our-latest-poll-findings-24 Tiny URL: **http://tinyurl.com/ls62htd**	
39	*2012 Edelman Trust Barometer* http://www.edelman.com/insights/intellectual-property/2012-edelman-trust-barometer/about-trust/executive-summary Tiny URL: **http://tinyurl.com/mhuas4r**	

40	**Gallup Poll:** *Trust in Government* http://www.gallup.com/poll/5392/trust-government.aspx Tiny URL: **http://tinyurl.com/bt3vylu**	
41	**Gallup Poll:** *U.S. Confidence in Organized Religion at Low Point* http://www.gallup.com/poll/155690/confidence-organized-religion-low-point.aspx Tiny URL: **http://tinyurl.com/79ahspy**	
42	**Gallup Poll:** *Americans' Confidence in Newspapers Continues to Erode* http://www.gallup.com/poll/163097/americans-confidence-newspapers-continues-erode.aspx Tiny URL: **http://tinyurl.com/kleddxf**	
43	**Gallup Poll:** *Americans' Confidence in Banks Falls to Record Low* http://www.gallup.com/poll/155357/americans-confidence-banks-falls-record-low.aspx Tiny URL: **http://tinyurl.com/6qxf6sd**	
44	*The Economics of Trust*, Tim Harford, *Forbes*, July 2010, http://www.forbes.com/2006/09/22/trust-economy-markets-tech_cx_th_06trust_0925harford.html Tiny URL: **http://tinyurl.com/mvsbtr**	

ASSESSMENTS

45	**Assess Your Organization,** is it a great place to work? http://www.greatplacetowork.com/our-services/assess-your-organization Tiny URL: **http://tinyurl.com/owkv38k**	
46	**Trust Quotient Assessment,** free short personal report, there is a fee for longer report http://trustsuite.trustedadvisor.com/ Tiny URL: **http://tinyurl.com/777x667**	
47	**The Trusted Leader Assessment,** free http://www.thetrustedleader.com/test.html Tiny URL: **http://tinyurl.com/bvv3tbp**	

VIDEO

| 48 | **Interview with Amy Lyman,** co-founder of The Great Place to Work Institute, on trustworthy leadership
http://www.youtube.com/watch?v=TAyyrc8F6fQ

Tiny URL: **http://tinyurl.com/k35ytks** | |

CHAPTER 8

Employing Appreciative Inquiry

Purpose and Outcomes

This chapter explores the benefits and practice of engaging in organizational and personal change from a positive world view rather than the traditional more negative method of problem identification and fixing. This relatively new field of Appreciative Inquiry (AI) has been applied to promote transformational change in many organizations around the world and has provided tangible benefits and generated excellent business results.

This overview of Appreciative Inquiry demonstrates that AI is relevant and successful for individuals, teams, and organizations, helping them to:

- develop positive communications about peak performance experiences through skilled questioning and listening
- identify and make explicit and visible the themes in these stories that constitute the *positive core* of strengths, values, and principles
- release creative and innovative energy by linking the *positive core* directly to the change agenda
- engage people in change that is both rewarding and energizing rather than demotivating, confusing, or uncertain

---

Appreciative Inquiry in Action

In 1991, Bliss Brown was working as a corporate banker in Chicago. She was also an Episcopal minister, mother of three children, and served on many civic organizations dedicated to improving life in Chicago. She found that these organizations – corporate, religious, and civic – did not share a common view or language as to what needed to be done to positively transform life and business in the city.

Becoming the positive force in change, she organized a conference in 1992 to answer important questions:

- *"What might happen if all of Chicago's citizens were encouraged to give public expression to their imagination about a healthy future for the city as a whole and were invited to claim their own role in bringing that vision to life?*
- *Is it not likely that giving public voice and support to deeply held civic visions will help create Chicago as a more vibrant home for the world's people?"*[76]

This conference gathered 65 Chicago leaders for two days, during which they were challenged to collectively envision a positive future for the city and all of its residents, as well as create an action plan to achieve that vision. What followed was extraordinary. Bliss left her 16 year career in banking within three days of the conference and pulled together a design team to use the principles of Appreciative Inquiry to crowdsource a broad, inter-organizational and inter-generational view of what people valued about Chicago and what type of future they wanted to co-create.

Three outcomes of this interview process were identified:

- **Creating a shared vision:** An *undivided Chicago conversation* seemed to nurture hope in the possibility of sharing ownership of the city's future.
- **Inter-generational appreciation**: The conversation opened lines of communication. Both the young people and the adults involved commented that they gained an appreciative understanding of the other generation.
- **Positive dialogue:** The conversation shifted away from problem-solving to collective visioning about a shared future, created energy, and opened new possibilities.

Just when I needed it most, IMAGINE CHICAGO provided a very positive outlook on how to view things in a positive way instead of negative. Through appreciative inquiry, it enabled

---

[76] Bliss W. Browne, "*A Chicago Case Study in Intergenerational Appreciative Inquiry,*" Imagine Chicago, AI Commons, 1999.

me to mobilize more effectively and to be able to get the most out of talking and working with people.
∞Yvonne Orr, The Woodlawn Organization

Appreciative Inquiry as a Positive Force in Change

Are organizations a problem that need to be fixed? This is the basic assumption of many leaders who apply problem-based management principles to align their organizations with the external environment. They are taught in business schools to identify problems, analyze causes, find solutions, and plan the implementation of the treatment to cure the problem.

Unfortunately, this deficit strategy has proven woefully inadequate for dealing with twenty-first century complexity and the sheer speed of change. The application of iterative, very narrow, slow fixes applied to large problems can only address the status quo. By the time you have fixed one problem, ten new problems have arrived. It's no surprise then that many become skeptical and/or often resist new (change) initiatives.

The brutal fact is that about 70 percent of all change initiatives fail.[77]
∞Michael Beer, professor emeritus, Harvard Business School, and Nitin Nohria, Dean, Harvard Business School

Resistance to change has been identified as a key factor in this failure. Therefore, traditional methods have also focused on overcoming resistance. But the bottom line is that change causes uncertainty and confusion, as well as anticipated loss for many in the organization. Therefore, it can easily lead to a negative culture, a disengaged workforce, and an overwhelming feeling that there are too many problems to be solved.

What would happen if organizations and humans were not seen as problems but as alive with infinite creative capacity just waiting to be realized? Appreciative Inquiry is founded on this viewpoint. In order to energize the latent capacity of people and organizations, the AI process crowdsources creative new solutions and innovations, leading to vibrant transformational change.

---

[77] Michael Beer and Nitin Nohria, "Cracking the Code of Change," *Harvard Business Review Press*, May (2000).

In the long run, what is more likely to be useful: Demoralizing a successful workforce by concentrating on their failures or helping them over their last few hurdles by building a bridge with their successes?

∞Tom White, President of GTE

What is Appreciative Inquiry (AI)?

Appreciative Inquiry begins with a positive perspective. It is a whole system view with a strengths-based approach to learning, discovery, and innovation. It seeks first and foremost to collectively uncover what is right with people and organizations. AI assumes that all organizations are social systems co-created by the members, and as such, change must be driven by all of the members of the system as they collaborate toward a common, meaningful goal.[78]

It is a combination of:

Appreciation:	Inquiry:
• to recognize the quality, significance or magnitude of • to be fully aware of or sensitive to • to raise in value or price	• to gather information for the purpose of learning and changing • to examine closely in a quest for truth

Table 3: Definition of Appreciative Inquiry

The Beginnings of Appreciative Inquiry

This first step of AI was uncovered serendipitously in 1985 by a team from The Weatherhead School of Management (Cleveland USA) led by David Cooperrider. While on a consulting engagement with the nearby Cleveland Clinic, Cooperrider's team asked the clinic's employees questions about the positive aspects of their work, and a groundswell of energy was uncovered.

Unintentionally, the team tapped into the organization's *positive core* by focusing everyone's attention on the positives about their work. The inquiry process alone generated more positivity, energy, engagement, and success. Thus, the Weatherhead team discovered one of the most important

---

[78] American Heritage Dictionary Online.

principles of AI – *that social systems grow in the direction of what they discuss, debate, and describe in dialogue and ongoing exchanges,* and based on this created the Appreciative Inquiry process for leading change.

The positive core is the collective wisdom, knowledge, strategies, attitudes, skills, and capabilities of the organization at its best.[79] It is what gives life and vitality to the organization.

In the affirmative inquiry process, people are asked to describe the experiences of peak performance and positive meaning at work. Encouraged to tell these stories, their attention is turned collectively toward strengths and excellence.

> *Perhaps it's obvious, but the process of doing the interviews is as important as the data collected.*
> ∞David Cooperrider, Fairmount Minerals Professor of Organizational Behavior at the Weatherhead School of Management at Case Western Reserve University and the creator of Appreciative Inquiry

Since that study, AI has grown as a comprehensive practice that is useful in individual coaching, team performance, and organizational transformational change. Many change practitioners and business and government leaders have actively employed the principles and methods of AI in creating large-scale change and bottom line results.

---

[79] David Cooperrider, Amanda Trosten-Bloom, and Diana Whitney, *The Power of Appreciative Inquiry (2nd Ed.),* (San Francisco: Berrett-Koehler, 2010).

John Deere	Green Mountain Coffee Roasters (GMCR)	Avon	Hunter Douglas
200 employees attended an AI Summit. Participants and management considered the large group conference an overwhelming success. Many participants shared that for the first time in 20 years, they now had hope for the future. Several teams worked on identifying the priority projects and successfully completed them within a month. One project alone returned a measurable $3 million in cost savings by reducing the cycle time of product introduction costs.	GMCR employed AI to help achieve the company's "25¢ Challenge," which was ultimately successful in reducing operating costs by 25 cents per pound of coffee, roughly a 7 percent reduction in gross costs. Among the improvements generated during GMCR's AI initiative was the adaptation of purchase orders for all buying activities, a change that cut costs in obtaining competitive bids and the processing of payables. The company also enhanced cash flow by optimizing its order entry and delivery systems, thus speeding the receipt of revenues.	Avon Mexico employed the AI process and discovered that men and women teamed best when they worked as co-chairs. Actively supporting this positive model, Avon experienced a major profit increase and won an award two years later as a best place for women to work.	In the first six months of the engagement, an Appreciative Inquiry was conducted with half of the existing workforce, along with a large representative sample of customers, suppliers, and community members. This inquiry ended with a 100-person Appreciative Inquiry Summit. In 2001, the Division estimated over $3.5 million in savings as a result of AI-based business process improvements during the previous 12 months.
"An Appreciative Inquiry Summit (AI Summit) at John Deere," Gina Hinrichs, Jim Ludema, Debbie Morris, AI Commons, 04/01/2000	*"The Art of Appreciative Inquiry,"* Theodore Kinni, Harvard Business School Working Knowledge for Business Leaders, 9/22/2003	*"AI in Diversity Work: Avon Mexico,"* Debbie Morris, Marge Schiller, AI Commons, January 2003	*"Creative AI Approaches for Whole-System Culture Change: Hunter Douglas Window Fashions Division,"* Amanda Trosten-Bloom, Diana Whitney, Corporation for Positive Change, AI Commons, 08/16/2001

Table 4: Organizations Using Appreciative Inquiry

How Can You Employ Appreciative Inquiry?

Appreciative Inquiry focuses attention on *"What is best in our current reality"* and *"What is possible in the future."* It's an emergent and iterative process of change that is achieved by pursuing recurring engagement of the five key steps: Define, Discover, Dream, Design, and Deliver.

AI engages people in a conscious choice to seek what is energizing, engaging, and life-affirming. It creates a context in which they can participate in building an organization where they want to work. It guides attention of the collective toward the best and highest qualities in themselves and the enterprise.

1. **Define**

   First, determine the theme for the appreciative inquiry.
   The process for selecting topics:
   • involves a cross-section of people from the organization and stakeholders
   • results from preliminary interviews
   • challenges people to reframe deficit issues into affirmative topics for inquiry

2. Discover

Focus on *"The best of what is"* and appreciate what is good and right in the current context. Interview people with a series of questions designed to bring to mind peak experiences, positive images, and a better future.

For example, when AI was used in Chicago to foster community, the questions included the following, among others:

IMAGINE CHICAGO CITYWIDE INTERVIEW QUESTIONS (1993-1994)[80]
- *"Thinking back over your Chicago memories, what have been real high points for you as a citizen of this city?*
- *Why did these experiences mean so much to you?*
- *How would you describe the quality of life in Chicago today?"*

In order to do this well, there must be agreement on the topic and the development of a draft interview protocol. Interviewers should be trained in attentive listening and provided with interview guidelines.

As you saw in the previous chart, Hunter Douglas interviewed half the workforce in this process. In fact, the more people involved when working on the Discover stage, the more you plant the seeds for positive change. A best practice used in AI Summits is pair interviews, using positive inquiry methods followed by work in small groups to identify themes that inform the positive core.

The goal is to create a collective narrative built on individual stories and images of what is truly strong, good, and positive about the past and present. This is not to say that the existence of problems should be ignored. The idea is to view problems through the lens of opportunity rather than the need to fix it, and bring together people, ideas, and resources to foster a potent force for change.

3. Dream

Dream about *"What might be."* Build on the outcomes and positive core themes found during the Discover phase so that people envision a future by articulating the dream or images of excellence.

---

[80] Bliss W. Browne, *"A Chicago Case Study in Intergenerational Appreciative Inquiry,"* Imagine Chicago, AI Commons, 1999.

This generates a broad range of possibilities, innovations, and creativity. For example, questions in the Imagine Chicago AI process included:[4]

- *"What changes in the city would you most like to see?*
  - *What do you imagine your own role might be in helping to make this happen?*
  - *Who could work with you?*

- *Close your eyes and imagine Chicago as you most want it to be a generation from now. What is it like? What do you see and hear? What are you proudest of having accomplished?"*

4. **Design**

Look at *"What should be."*

Unfortunately, here is where many groups jump to Delivery. Unless the collective group co-creates the view of the ideal future firmly rooted in shared values and principles, there is a strong potential for a sliding back to old processes and structures.

Instead, define and prioritize the opportunities and potential pathways. For example, a new organization design could be developed, tapping into the positive core and helping to realize the expressed dream.

5. **Deliver (Destiny)**

Create a destiny based on *"What will be."*

During this stage, the future is brought to life. The new approaches, processes, systems, organization designs, etc. are implemented. It's important to also think about how to sustain momentum for ongoing positive change and performance.

The Appreciative Inquiry process can be used in individual coaching, to enable teams and departments to meet challenges and implement large-scale organizational transformational change. (see Chapter 9: Coaching for Positive Change)

The AI process conveys:
- the power of affirmative questions to drive change
- the function of human narrative in creating social systems

- the benefit of creating alignment across multiple boundaries

Most importantly, AI has the ability to create flexible, adaptive, and innovative organizations that are equipped to rapidly meet the challenges of the twenty-first century.

> *Once you get this process going, people have this 'A-ha' experience. They have wanted a different kind of workplace, one that provides fulfillment and inspiration as well as a pay-check. Appreciative Inquiry gives them that, and it makes them the primary means by which it's created.*
> ∞ Jane Whatkins [81]

Resources for You to Employ Appreciative Inquiry

The useful and informative resources below will help you to understand and leverage Appreciative Inquiry in your work and life.

Recommended Books

Appreciative Inquiry: A Positive Approach to Building Cooperative Capacity, Barrett, F.J. & Fry, R.E. Chagrin Falls, OH: Taos Institute, FIRST EDITION, 2005
   o A precise introduction of the practice of Appreciative Inquiry. Offers good insights into mobilizing rapid, positive change with multiple stakeholders in a human system.

Appreciative Inquiry Handbook: For Leaders of Change (2nd ed.), Cooperrider, D.L., Whitney, D. & Stavros, J.M., Crown Custom Publishing, 2008
   o An in-depth explanation of what AI is and how it works, and includes stories of AI interventions and classic articles, sample project plans, interview guidelines, participant worksheets, a list of resources, a glossary of terms, and more.

---

[81] Ralph Kelly, Bernard J. Mohr, Jane Magruder Watkins, *Appreciative Inquiry: Change at the Speed of Imagination, Practicing Organization Development, Vol. 35*, John Wiley & Sons, 2011.

The Thin Book of Appreciative Inquiry (3rd ed.), Hammond, S.A., Bend: Thinbook Publisher, 2013

- o An introduction to the exciting organizational change philosophy called Appreciative Inquiry, showing ways of thinking, seeing and acting to drive purposeful change in organizations. Especially useful in situations that demand speedy, transformational change.

The Appreciative Inquiry Summit: A Practitioner's Guide for Leading Large Group Change, **Ludema**, J.D. Whitney, D., Mohr, B.J. & Griffen, T.J., Berrett-Koehler, 2003

- o Describes the process in use to design, guide and lead an Appreciative Inquiry Summit. It includes ample templates, guidelines and key concepts, enhanced by stories of successful summits and their results.

Articles, Research, Newsletters & Video

ARTICLES & RESEARCH	URL	QR CODE IMAGE
49	Graduate Studies, research, and executive education www.cwru.edu Tiny URL: **http://tinyurl.com/kkebryd**	
50	**Corporation for Positive Change** www.positivechange.com Tiny URL: **http://tinyurl.com/ka9mt2e**	
51	Articles, samples and case studies about AI http://ai.cwru.edu Tiny URL: **http://tinyurl.com/l7sz5rx**	
52	Tips, research and tools for **AI Practitioner** and newsletters www.aipractitioner.com Tiny URL: **http://tinyurl.com/oclupus**	
53	**Appreciative Inquiry** articles, news, applications http://guides.lib.unc.edu/AI **http://tinyurl.com/lr6jfld**	

VIDEOS	URL	QR CODE IMAGE
54	**What is Appreciative Inquiry?** A learning video http://www.youtube.com/watch?v=QzW22wwh1J4 Tiny URL: **http://tinyurl.com/qaf6xhx**	
55	An interview with David Cooperrider, a founder of the practice of Appreciative Inquiry http://www.youtube.com/watch?v=3JDfr6KGV-k Tiny URL: **http://tinyurl.com/l82slk8**	

CHAPTER 9

Coaching for Positive Change

Purpose and Outcomes

This chapter explains the positive impact of a coaching mind-set and a coaching culture to twenty-first century organizations in:
- fostering engagement and retention
- improving self-awareness and self-management
- creating a climate of performance support, motivation and positivity
- embedding a solutions and results-focus in the organizational culture
- overcoming resistance to change

Sunil is a highly talented engineer who was working for a large IT company as an embedded consultant with one of their major clients. Dissatisfied with his growth opportunities in his role, he enrolled in an Executive Master's Business Administration (EMBA) program, while continuing to work as an IT professional and caring for his young family.

Midway through the two year EMBA program, Sunil felt stuck. He could not see how what he was learning was going to propel his career in a direction that would resonate with his desires for the future. He was thinking of quitting the EMBA and had begun to apply unsuccessfully to other companies for work that was very similar to his current employment. It was suggested to him that engaging an Executive Coach might be helpful in his search to define a career pathway where he could grow, and fully engage his interests and emotional energy.

Sunil found an Executive Coach. Working with his coach, he reviewed the results of his Leadership 360°, gained more understanding of his strengths and personality style, and explored ideas and actions he had taken in pursuit of potential future careers. Finally, after taking a career assessment, he discovered that his strongest interests were in entrepreneurial activities. In the discussion of the results with his coach, he explained that he had grown up in a village outside a large city in India, and every member of his family had launched and run a successful business.

It was like a sudden bright light illuminating a future that made sense. Sunil realized that he would never thrive in a large bureaucratic, hierarchical organization, but wanted the excitement, flexibility and drive of creating and running his own business. With his attention now in a sharp focus on a specific goal, he got to work gathering the ideas and resources he needed to launch a business. He was selected as one of the EMBA students in his class to present his business plan to venture capitalists in a Shark Tank presentation.[82] It was successful.

Sunil completed his EMBA and launched his new business.

Coaching as a Positive Force in Change

We now accept the fact that learning is a lifelong process of keeping abreast of change. And the most pressing task is to teach people how to learn.
∞Peter Drucker, Claremont Graduate University
professor and management guru

To survive in the global economy, people and enterprises must be flexible, adaptable and growing in ways not previously experienced. Because of this, most organizations are experiencing major and minor change initiatives at the same time with significant impact on their employees. And, the pace of this change is not slowing but accelerating.

As we discussed in several other chapters in this book, the changing nature of work, the workforce, and demands of the global economy have dramatically altered the style of leadership required. No more *command and control.*

---

[82] In a TV show called *Shark Tank*, entrepreneurs pitch their business ideas to millionaire and billionaire investors in the hopes of securing funding to start, grow or save their business.

If not command and control based on a nineteenth century military model, what are the capabilities required of skillful leaders in the knowledge economy?

First and foremost, the twenty-first century leader must be a curious learner who asks the type of questions that *broaden and build*[83] and listens deeply to possibilities and opportunities in the responses. These leaders are able to harmonize diverse perspectives in the midst of complexity in ways that make sense to themselves and others.

The rapid and unexpected shifts in today's world demand leaders who are willing to pose questions and collaborate with their executives and peers in a manner that reduces friction, enhancing productivity and results. These leaders themselves must be adaptable in change, at times leaving their preferred style, and taking on a style that will lead to inspiration, alignment, purpose and meaning.

This requires a coaching mind-set, driven by a spirit of positive inquiry, where the leader asks insightful questions thereby building a relationship of openness and trust. This coaching mind-set in the leader helps others to be focused in-the-moment and to uncover innovative individual and collective solutions to challenges. Then they are enabled to perceive, define and master the change that is demanded.

> *One key to successful leadership is continuous personal change. Personal change is a reflection of our inner growth and empowerment.*
> ∞Robert E. Quinn, University of Michigan faculty member and director Center for Positive Organizational Scholarship

The coaching approach results in change that is positive, not resisted, because it is not driven from above, but through the adoption and adaptation to the change by the individuals responsible for its successful execution. Putting the strength of coaching behind strategy execution ensures that dialogue and problem resolution takes place when and where it is most needed.

---

[83] This research by Barbara L. Fredrickson is discussed in the Chapter 2: Fostering Optimism and Positivity.

What is Coaching for Positive Change?

The evolution of coaching and changes in business practices parallel each other. In late twentieth century business, there was an advent of flattened hierarchies and the kaleidoscopic changes in organizational structures. These changes have increased demand for collaboration, teamwork, emotional intelligence, and interpersonal/behavioral skills. Leaders who tended in the past toward a more autocratic style were forced to adapt... and in some cases needed coaching assistance to make the transition. This was a remedial rationale for an executive coach in business.

Then the pace of change increased exponentially and in the twenty-first century businesses found that they needed to accelerate the development of leadership capability throughout their newly global workforce. Now coaching was used to build the requisite skills faster than learning over time and from experience could provide. Coaches were hired to build competence in behavioral skill gaps and to develop cross-cultural capabilities in the high potential talent, grooming them to climb the career ladder more quickly. Both the remedial and the high potential types of coaching continue today.

However, more recently, a coach approach and mind-set has been used as an organizational development strategy. By embedding coaching as a daily interpersonal practice among the members of the workforce, organizations are seeking to build a worldwide alignment of engagement, positivity, and on-the-job apprenticeship. Research has found that coaching can maintain high performance in the midst of complexity, chaos and change.

A coaching culture in an organization *"increases focus on developing others and managing performance; increases sharing and utilization of knowledge; leads to more participative and transparent decision-making; and makes learning and development a top priority."*[84]

---

[84] *2009 Survey of Business Leaders,* Center for Creative Leadership.

What is Coaching?

Coaching is a synthesis of understandings, models and research from various fields including consulting, adult learning, psychology, change management, training, neuroscience and systems thinking, among others. Because coaching practice today draws from so many fields it can also mean different things to different people.

However, we find the definition of coaching by the International Coach Federation (ICF) to be the most reflective of today's practice of coaching. On their website, they state *"coaching is partnering with clients in a thought-provoking and creative process that inspires them to maximize their personal and professional potential"*. Under this umbrella, there are many types of coaching specific to targeted needs: executive coach, life coach, drama coach, sports coach, etc., all focused on improving performance.

For our consideration, the differences in business among managing, coaching, mentoring, training and therapy are especially relevant.

	MANAGING	COACHING	MENTORING	TRAINING	THERAPY
MINDSET	Task assignment	Collaborative, creative goal attainment	Expertise and insight sharing	Teaching	Healing
STATEMENT	'This is your job...'	'How can I support you..."	'This is how I would do it...'	'Let me teach you how...'	'Tell me about yourself...'
BEHAVIOR	· Motivating · Monitoring · Evaluating	· Exploration · Building new ways of being and thinking	· Advice · Guidance	· Teach tools, methods, processes	· Question · Psychoanalyze · Reflection

So coaching is not therapy, nor is it managing. However, all of these roles might at times employ coaching as a mind-set and a set of skills to build individual and team performance.

The role of the coach is to:

- build a relationship of trust and openness
- focus on the coachee
- appreciate the coachee's strengths, values, goals and perspective
- provide a place where the coachee can gain clarity by hearing their own voice
- pose questions that drive new thinking and potential actions

- listen with intention and reflect what is heard
- facilitate positive change
- be confidential

Coaching attributes and skills include questioning and listening skills, empathy, curiosity, and mindfulness – being in-the-moment, brain chatter turned off and non-judgmental. Utilizing these skills, a coach helps others to:

- define who they want to be
- recognize what really interests and matters to them
- deal with stress and change
- leverage their strengths
- overcome things that seem to be obstacles
- recognize and alter negativity and self-limiting thought patterns
- become their best-realized selves
- build stronger relationships

In coaching for positive change, there are some important keys to success. Every professional business coach should be certified, credible and competent. If the goal is to embed coaching in everyday interactions on-the-job, training in coaching is required for all managers. Also, for a successful coaching experience, the synergy in the coaching relationship must be positive.

The Coaching Process

Whether a manager is using a coaching approach to motivate high performance or it is a professional coach, the coach must first build belief that the coaching sessions will generate value for the coachee. Immediately, the coach must establish a strong relationship with the coachee. During the first coaching session (ideally in person), it is important for the coach to build the trust by explaining their role, the role of the coachee, and especially the fact that all coaching discussions between them are highly confidential.

Next, it is helpful to acquire input from a 360° Assessment, so that the coachee can gain more specific information on what would be most valuable for them to put into focus. Assessments of emotional intelligence, leadership practices, career preferences, personality style, and values and strengths are incredibly helpful in this clarification process, establishing a sense of self-awareness and knowledge. Sometimes the assessment(s) are selected by the organization. For other coaching engagements, the coach might identify those assessments that will generate the most relevant insights, as was the case with Sunil in the opening of this chapter.

Many times, it is helpful to start with just one assessment, especially a 360° and then as the coaching process unfolds, introduce additional assessments just-in-time as they are of interest.

Positive Methods for Performance Data Gathering

In order to set goals for the coaching, it is critical to gather performance data. The two most popular positive methods for gathering performance data, include the **Feed Forward** process, and the **Best Reflected Self** exercise.

Feed Forward

A highly positive improvement was created by Marshall Goldsmith. He calls this the *feed forward* technique. Realizing that high performers do not like to receive *feedback* – in fact nobody does – because it focuses solely on the negative and doesn't offer a solution. Goldsmith designed a real-time dialogue-based 360° process that begins by gathering and summarizing performance data in a standard 360° assessment from multiple stakeholders. After reviewing the report, the coach helps the coachee reflect on the various potential areas for improvement.

Then, the client selects a performance goal – *to be more collaborative* – for example. This goal is shaped by the client as a question, e.g. *"How can I become more collaborative?"*

They are instructed to go out into their lives and ask everyone around them this question, getting their responses. When the response is given, they are not to dispute it or disregard it, but write it down and say *"Thank you"*. These stakeholders, who initially offered their ideas for improvement, then become their accountability partners, since they have given their advice and are now watching for results. Finally, all of this input is reviewed with the coach and specific action plans are created. A month later, the coachee goes around again to the same stakeholders and asks, *"Do you have any more ideas for me?"* This process makes their effort visible to others, and provides a positive path to performance improvement.[85]

This same process can be employed very effectively by a manager who is using the coaching approach. It puts the coachee in charge of and responsible for their own performance goals and outcomes.

Best Reflected Self

Another positive process for gathering 360° information is the *Best Reflected Self* exercise, created by Robert Quinn and others at the University of Michigan.[86] The coachee gathers information from others about the times when the coachee was performing at their best. This is gathered and analyzed in two phases, leading to a personal development action plan that is inspired by the new insights of the individual at their best.

In Phase 1, the coachee creates a *Best Reflected Self* profile by selecting 15 – 20 respondents and asking them to provide them with three stories of when they were at their best, identifying specifically their positive contribution at that time. The coachee is also asked to reflect on their personal perspective of when they were performing at their best. They then aggregate and analyze the stories, identifying patterns and themes. Finally, they compose a Best Reflected Self-portrait in writing.

In Phase 2, the focus for the coaching is on creating an Action Plan, bringing the Best Reflected Self to life by reflecting on how the coachee can best use the information gathered to enhance the quality of their work and life, to leverage their best self in their current work, to build positive relationships and future career plans, and to identify the situations that will foster their growth and development.

Once the goals for the coaching are in a clear line-of-sight, the coaching takes on a different perspective, asking questions such as:

- *How will you get there?*
- *How will you maintain the positive energy to keep going when it seems tough?*

---

[85] Marshall Goldsmith, *What Got You Here Won't Get You There*, Hyperion, New York, 2007, pp170-176.
[86] Robert Quinn, Jane Dutton, Gretchen Spreitzer and Laura Roberts, *Best Reflected Self*, Regents of the University of Michigan, 2011.

- *What are your purposes and passions and how are these reflected in your goal(s)?*
- *What experiences have you had in the past that can assist you in taking action?*
- *How can you leverage each of your strengths to achieve your goal(s)?*
- *What resources do you have in your life that can support you?*

This is a positive approach applied to focus on solutions and results, not barriers, challenges and obstacles, and again can be employed both by managers and coaches with their coachees.

Coaching Models

GROW Model

There are many models for coaching, and one of the most popular is the GROW model – Goal, Reality, Options, and Will (or *what will you do?*), developed by Sir John Whitmore.[87]

- **GOAL** addresses areas to work on, desired outcomes, expectations, objectives, steps to take to reach a goal, and so on.
- **REALITY** addresses the present situation, who is affected, personal control over outcomes, action steps taken so far, obstacles, resources, and so on.
- **OPTIONS** addresses different ways to approach something, alternatives, impact of budget, advantages and disadvantages, solutions with the most appeal, most satisfactory ideas, and so on.
- **WILL** (What Will You Do?) addresses choosing an option or options, how well it matches objectives, critical success factors, potential hindrances, personal resistance, level of commitment, levels of support, and so on.

---

[87] Sir John Whitmore, *Coaching for Performance: Growing People, Performance, and Purpose,* Nicolas Brealy Publishing, 2002.

The GROW Model		
Acronym	Description	Example Questions
G – Goal	Coachee is asked to clarify what they want to achieve from each session. Determines the focus of the coaching.	*What do you want to achieve this session?* *How would you like to feel afterward?* *What would be the best use of this time?*
R – Reality	Raise awareness of present realities. Examine how current situation is impacting coachee's goals.	*How have things gone in the past week?* *How have you handled any problems?* *What worked, what didn't work?*
O – Options	Identify and assess available options. Encourage solution-focused thinking and brainstorming.	*What possible options do you have?* *What has worked for you in the past?* *What haven't you tried yet that might work?*
W – Wrap-up	Assists the coachee to determine next steps. Develops an action plan and builds motivation.	*What is the most important thing to do next?* *What might get in the way?* *Who might be able to support you?* *How will you feel when this is done?*

Table 5: The GROW Model:
Sources: Grant & Grant 2004; Landsberg 1997; Whitmore, 1992

Appreciative Inquiry Coaching

One of the most interesting new coaching models is described by Orem, et al, in their book, *Appreciative Coaching: A Positive Process for Change.*[88]

In their book, the authors merge the 4-D process (Discover, Dream, Design, Destiny) of appreciative inquiry (See the Chapter 8: Employing Appreciative Inquiry) with questions that focus the individual on answers that reflect positive situations, experiences, achievements, strengths and values. This moves the attention of the coachee from a negative process of looking at and solving problems, toward positive possibilities and creative ways to achieve the future vision.

---

[88] Sara L. Orem, Jacqueline Binkert, Ann Clancy. 2007, *Appreciative Coaching: A Positive Process for Change*, Josey Bass, A Wiley Imprint.

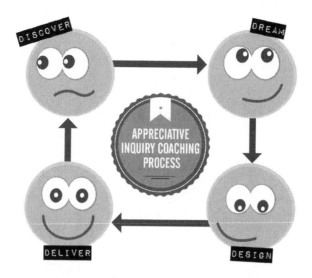

Discover

The appreciative inquiry process begins with identifying the best of what has been or what is. The coach requests that the client develop the answers to several appreciative questions...already reframing their expectations of what the coaching will be about. This includes questions such as:

- *What have been your three greatest accomplishments in your life?*
- *What aspects of your life do you find most enjoyable?*
- *Who have been your major role models, and what about them do you find admirable?*

Dream

Next, during the dream stage the coachee is supported to envision a meaningful future, creating a self-image so powerful that it inspires and motivates them to move toward that dream.

Design

During this phase, the coachee's focus is directed toward proactively attaining the dream. Specific actions are made and reviewed for key learning and insight.

Destiny

Life is a constant process of creation. This phase is about living a life fully realized, drawing the coachee's attention to how they are achieving their dream in the present moment, enabling them to sustain the momentum for ongoing positive change and high performance.

There are many reasons for utilizing the principles of appreciative inquiry in the coaching relationship. Neuroscience has found that what we focus on actually has significant impact on the brain, this is called neuroplasticity. (Read more about this in Chapter 1: The Neuroscience of Leading Positive Change) The brain changes to absorb the information and emotions being noticed. Also, it is well known that what we focus on increases our attentiveness to learning and opportunities in the area under consideration. In addition, positive psychologists have found that valuing enjoyable experiences is a critical key to happiness.

Coaches applying positive inquiry methods encourage coachees to focus on the things that are right with their world and support the coachee in valuing and leveraging their best experiences, strengths, values and visions in the creation of a positive future.

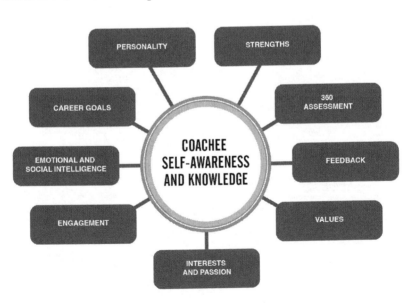

Miracles happen everyday, change your perception of what a miracle is and you'll see them all around you.
∞ Jon Bon Jovi, singer, philanthropist, and actor

Resources for Exploration and Learning

Recommended Books

Appreciative Coaching: A Positive Process for Change. Sara L. Orem, Jacqueline Binkert, Ann Clancy. 2007, Josey Bass, A Wiley Imprint
- o The authors describe in great detail the benefits of leveraging the process of appreciative inquiry in coaching. They give examples of how this approach supports coachees in rediscovering their own sense of excitement and energy in their life and future opportunities.

What Got You Here Won't Get You There, Marshall Goldsmith, Hyperion, New York, 2007, pp170-176
- o Goldsmith gives an excellent description of how he leverages the Feed Forward concept in his coaching practice.

Coaching for Leadership: The Practice of Leadership Coaching from the World's Greatest Coaches, Marshall Goldsmith, Laurence Lyons, editors, John Wiley and Sons 2006
- o The world's greatest coaches, including, among others: Marshall Goldsmith, Paul Hersey, Beverly Kay, David Ulrich, offer the world-class best practices they use in their executive coaching practice.

Coaching Corporate MVPs: Challenging and Developing High-Potential Employees. Margaret Butteriss, Right Management, Josey-Bass, 2008
- o A comprehensive guide to identify the Most Valuable Players (MVPs) in your organization and to put into place a plan to develop this talent at all levels with a customized coaching approach.

Coaching Successfully, John Eaton, Roy Johnson, Dorling Kindersley, 2000
- o The Essential Manager series offers precise descriptions of dozens of business techniques, skills, and methods, amplified by photos, charts, and diagrams. Quick and to the point, it gives busy managers who want to use a coaching approach lots of tools to be successful.

Coaching for Performance: Growing People, Performance, and Purpose,
Sir John Whitmore, Nicolas Brealy Publishing, 2002
- o   In a clear and precise guide, this book describes the foundations of coaching, and the GROW model in depth with coaching questions and chapters on the role of emotional intelligence and leadership.

Article, Assessment & Training

ARTICLE	URL	QR CODE IMAGE
56	*Appreciative Inquiry Coaching Paper,* Sandy Gordon, International Coaching Psychology Review, Vol. 3 No. 1, March 2008, pp. 17 – 29. The author describes the core principles, generic process and psychological foundations of Appreciative Inquiry and offers excellent questions to use in the AI coaching process http://www.instituteofcoaching.org/images/ARticles/ICPR_AI_coaching_paper.pdf Tiny URL: **http://tinyurl.com/nzl53h3**	
ASSESSMENT		
57	*The Best Reflected Self Exercise* is available for sale as a PDF download at the website of the Center for Positive Organizations http://positiveorgs.bus.umich.edu/cpo-tools/reflected-best-self-exercise-2nd-edition/ Tiny URL: **http://tinyurl.com/k4stvnl**	
TRAINING		
58	**Appreciative Inquiry Coach Training (AICT),** approved by the International Coach Federation (ICF) for Continuing Coach Education Units (CCEUs) trains coaches in the art of applying appreciative inquiry principles into their coaching relationships, is comprised of a 5 day residential program, plus a practicum. http://www.centerforappreciativeinquiry.net/offering/appreciative-inquiry-coaching-training-aict/ Tiny URL: **http://tinyurl.com/lmcchac**	

CHAPTER 10

The Future Now

Purpose and Outcomes

This chapter is a look into the future of leading positive change and how you can begin to harness the amazing science and practices described in the themes of the book .

Create tomorrow today!

There are incredible opportunities to do things differently. Finally we have the solid basis of research and data to support success in leading positive change. Now we know more about what works, and what doesn't, and why.

> *Managers who understand the recent breakthroughs in cognitive science can lead and influence mindful change: organizational transformation that takes into account the physiological nature of the brain, and the ways in which it predisposes people to resist some forms of leadership and accept others.*
>
> ∞David Rock, founder and CEO of Results Coaching Systems (RCS), and Jeffrey Schwartz, American psychiatrist and researcher in the field of neuroplasticity

Every human has an extraordinary potential to embrace life, to contribute value, and to make a difference. Hard science is now providing insights into what makes it possible to realize the full value of that talent in each person. We have gained amazing insights into how to organize, motivate, manage, and reward effort to achieve positive outcomes and solid results. Based on these findings, the fields of psychology, management, education, and sociology are already offering methods, processes and tools to integrate these findings into our everyday work and life.

Now that brain science can follow the pattern of a thought as it circulates through the brain, like tracing the flow of blood as it flows through the body, the pattern of analyzing and responding to change is demonstrated to be universal and predictable. The brain resists it. Logic might accept that the change is needed but the hard-wiring in the brain actively works against it.

This is because change is deeply challenging on the emotional level. The orbital frontal cortex lights up when something different occurs from what is expected. This automatic reaction in the brain is closely linked to the amygdala, inciting perceptions of danger and feelings of fear. In turn, these two areas of the brain draw energy and resources from the pre-frontal cortex – the executive center of the brain – responsible for higher level intellectual, and logical thinking.[89] Thus, when leaders announce change, the collective organizational brain sends strong *error* messages, limiting the ability to adapt and implement change.

But change is coming fast and in unexpected and unpredictable forms. Thus, the capacity for organizations to master frequent transformational change is more urgent every year. Just changing the systems, processes, methods, and policies in an organization, although a step in the right direction, is a totally inadequate approach to address the challenges of adaptive and flexible change. The human talent in an organization must be fully engaged with **hearts and minds** to accept and drive the change.

When leaders understand and leverage the positive mental and emotional forces that overcome the natural resistance to change, the new insights and actions can be hardwired into the collective organizational brain.

Some of the key principles that support leading positive change include:

- **Inner strengths** – values, mental capabilities and talents – are innate and genetic and are an enduring source of well-being
- **True motivation** – derives not from 'if you do this, then you get a reward', but when the reason for doing something is the joy of the effort and is linked with personal purpose and passion

---

[89] David Rock and Jeffrey Schwartz, The Neuroscience of Leadership, strategy + business, May 2006.

- **Trust** – deactivates the 'fear center' of the brain, and supports optimal brain function
- **Appreciation for the good** – drives out negative thinking and builds new positive neural pathways in the brain
- **Social support** – the mirror neurons in the brain reflect the tone and pace of those around us, if the culture is dynamic, energizing and engaging, the brain resonates with positive thoughts and ultimately action
- **Emotions** – can be elevated from the negative to the positive by using self-directed neuroplasticity to move from quick negative reactions, to reflection-guided elevation of the emotions followed by action
- **Calming the mind** – supports emotional awareness and clear thinking
- **Centering in the positive core** – creates an optimistic virtuous circle in the brain that fosters feelings of safety, strength, accomplishment, gratitude and resilience

Long ago, Aristotle contributed much to this field and coined the word *eudemonia*, which derives from the Greek words *eu* (good) and *daimōn* (spirit). His work describes happiness in its deepest sense, that of the highest human good and a sense of flourishing.

Happiness is the meaning and the purpose of life, the whole aim and end of human existence.
∞Aristotle, Greek philosopher and scientist, 384–322 BCE

Recently, in a discussion with an executive who had graduated from Harvard, he was asked *"What was the most subscribed course when you were a student?"* He immediately said Econ 10. Things have changed a lot in the past 30 years! Interestingly, in November 2011, dozens of students walked out of Econ 10 in protest for what they perceived as a limited view of economics. *"Their specific criticisms were that economics as taught in this class, formally called Economics 10, failed to prevent the financial crisis and does nothing to narrow the gap between rich and poor."*[90] Now the most subscribed course at Harvard is no longer Econ 10, but it is Dr. Tal Ben-

---

[90] Amity Shlaes, *Harvard's Walkout Students Misunderstand Economics,* Bloomberg View, November 10, 2011.

Shahar's Positive Psychology course called PSY 1504 that teaches students how to be happy!

Attaining lasting happiness requires that we enjoy the journey on our way toward a destination we deem valuable. Happiness, therefore, is not about making it to the peak of the mountain, nor is it about climbing aimlessly around the mountain: happiness is the experience of climbing toward the peak.
∞Tal Ben-Shahar, teacher and author, co-founder of the Whole Being Institute

In his book, *Happier: Learn the Secrets to Daily Joy and Lasting Fulfillment,* he identifies a set of principles that can help you to open the positivity in your heart and mind. Shawn Achor, a psychology student and then educator and researcher at Harvard, has also contributed much to the steps needed to attain happiness, and describes seven similar practices that support success and performance at work.[91] These include:

1. **The Happiness Advantage** – A positive brain thinks better than one in neutral or locked in negativity. Neuroplasticity proves that our brains can be changed for the better!

2. **The Fulcrum and the Lever** – Our mind-set has control over how we perceive the world and events around us. A positive mind-set (the fulcrum) gives the power (the lever) to experience more fulfillment and success.

3. **The Tetris Effect** – The brain can be retrained to see possibilities and opportunities, rather than negativity, failure and stress.

4. **Falling Up** – The path to learn positive lessons from adversity or defeat, creating a mental map to more success and happiness, even in bad experiences.

5. **The Zorro Circle** – The brain is more responsive to small, manageable goals that gradually with practice and exercise can be expanded into ever larger circles.

6. **The 20 Second Rule** – By making small energy adjustments to feed positivity in the brain, old negative thinking and behaviors can be changed.

---

[91] Shawn Achor, *The Happiness Advantage: The Seven Principles that Fuel Success and Performance at Work*, Virgin Books, 2010, pp. 17 - 18.

7. **Social Investment** – Positive relationships in our social support network are the most important predictors of success and excellence.

The field continues to expand just about every day! Seligman has challenged his own early theories of happiness and pushed the envelope even further in his new book, *Flourish*, where he identifies the core five elements of well-being[92] – a combination of feeling good or being happy, as well as experiencing engagement and the joy of having meaning, good relationships and accomplishment. We can choose the course in our lives to maximize all of these. Well-being is supported by:

*   **Positive Emotions** (which include *happiness*)
*   **Engagement** – the sense of being totally lost in the enjoyment of a task
*   **Relationships** – not just your sense of how you feel about others in your life, but how others feel about you
*   **Meaning** – the degree to which you actually serve something larger than self
*   **Achievement** – you have achieved your goals and they have a positive impact on the people you care about and the world.

The topic of positive psychology is well-being, the gold standard for measuring well-being is flourishing, and the goal of positive psychology is to increase flourishing.
∞Martin E.P. Seligman, psychologist, educator, author and Director
of the Positive Psychology Center, University of Pennsylvania

The focus on measuring well-being is increasing. Gallup conducts an annual global well-being poll that measures the percentage of the population 150 countries around the world on who are *Thriving, Struggling,* or *Suffering.* Based on the Cantril Self-Anchoring Striving Scale, participants in each country are asked to rate their personal present and future lives on a 0 to 10 scale. A '0' is the worst possible life and a '10' the best possible life. Each year Gallup conducts this poll and publishes the results with indications whether the scales have moved up or down compared to the prior year.

---

[92] Martin E.P. Seligman, *Flourish: A Visionary New Understanding of Happiness and Well-being,* Free Press, 2011, pp 23 - 27.

Interesting results show that compared to the other regions, the African countries fall lowest on the *thriving* scale, with Malawi ranked the highest and Togo the lowest. Whereas, European countries rank the highest overall, with Denmark on the top and Bulgaria the lowest ranked. Countries in Asia, with New Zealand at the top and Cambodia at the bottom, and the Americas, with Costa Rica at the top and Haiti at the bottom, are pretty much in the same positions on the *thriving* scale. Gallup hopes that this with other metrics will give guidance to global leaders on what needs to happen to improve the quality of life for their residents. It would be highly interesting to use this process in assessing the well-being of employees in organizations!

> *The official metrics for global wellbeing are done. This new institution of behavioral economic data will forever change how world leaders lead.*
> ∞ Jim Clifton, Gallup CEO

What's Next?

Begin your positive journey today! With changes you personally accomplish toward a goal of positive transformation of yourself, you will be able to support the transformation of others, your teams, your organization and the world.

> *There is no passion to be found playing small – in settling for a life that is less than the one you are capable of living.*
> ∞ Nelson Mandela, President of South Africa, 1994-1999

Resources for Exploration and Learning

These resources will help you to further understand how you can take steps to move into realizing more happiness and enjoyment in your future life and work.

Recommended Books

Choose the Life You Want: The Mindful Way to Happiness, Tal Ben-Shahar, The Experiment LLC, 2012

- ○ Ben-Shahar uses recent brain research findings to demonstrate how we can make the right choices, small ones we make every day, to make conscious choices for a happy and fulfilled life.

The Happiness Advantage: The Seven Principles that Fuel Success and Performance at Work, Shawn Achor, Virgin Books, 2010

- ○ The recent brain research and psychology of happiness indicate that we have it wrong. It was always thought that *If* we can just find that great job, win that next promotion, lose those five pounds, happiness will follow. But this formula is actually backward: Happiness fuels success, not the other way around. Achor gives a lively view of 7 principles to drive positivity and happiness by using brain power!

Flourish: A Visionary New Understanding of Happiness and Well-being, Martin E.P. Seligman, Free Press, 2011

- ○ In a fascinating evolution of thought and practice, *Flourish* refines what Positive Psychology is all about. Initially Seligman focused on happiness and optimism, and now has come to realize and here explains that there is more to human well-being and a life that promotes flourishing.

The Neuroscience of Leadership, David Rock and Jeffrey Schwartz, strategy + business, May 2006

- ○ Breakthroughs in brain research are employed to offer ways to make organizational transformation succeed.

Switch: How to change things when change is hard, Chip and Dan Heath, Random House Business Books, 2010

- ○ Using human behavior and the brain research to offer powerful solutions that actually work.

Lift: Becoming a Positive Force in Any Situation, Ryan W. Quinn, Robert E. Quinn, Berrett Koehler Publishers Inc., 2009
- o Offers four important questions, exercises and tools based on neuroscience and social sciences that can give a *lift* in any situation.

Article and Videos

ARTICLE	URL	QR CODE IMAGE
59	*Global Wellbeing: The Behavioral Economics of GDP Growth* http://www.gallup.com/poll/126965/gallup-global-wellbeing.aspx Tiny URL:**http://tinyurl.com/nrxp2ch**	
VIDEOS		
60	Tal Ben-Shahar, *Happiness 101* http://www.youtube.com/watch?v=5-RVECUWOGQ Tiny URL: **http://tinyurl.com/cl5pbgy**	
61	Big Think *Interview with Tal Ben-Shahar* http://bigthink.com/users/talbenshahar Tiny URL: **http://tinyurl.com/phttaws**	
62	Shawn Achor, *The Happy Secret to Better Work* http://www.ted.com/talks/shawn_achor_the_happy_secret_to_better_work?language=en Tiny URL: **http://tinyurl.com/ozcyejz**	
63	On a lighter note...**The Happy Song**, Pharrell Williams https://www.youtube.com/watch?v=y6Sxv-sUYtM Tiny URL: **http://tinyurl.com/l9mwz4q**	

About the Authors

Eileen McDonough Rogers

Ms. Rogers is a highly experienced professional in the field of executive and leadership development. Currently the CEO and founder of LeadershipSigma® (www.leadershipsigma.com), an international leadership development consulting firm. Ms. Rogers served recently as Vice President, Global Talent Solutions, Berlitz, and prior to that as Global Director, Leadership and Talent Excellence, Deloitte, with responsibility to create and implement global strategic initiatives for leadership and management development, including designing and teaching leadership courses around the world. She has created award winning blended learning experiences for managers and executives including: e-learning, virtual classroom, face-to-face, virtual coaching and Internet supported action learning projects.

Other highlights include: Director of Executive Education Programs at Harvard University, Babson College, and Boston University, directing teams responsible for executive and leadership development programs in corporations, including global Fortune 100 firms based in Europe, the US and Asia Pacific; public organizations; and academic institutions. In these capacities she has joined together faculty from major US business schools as well as IMD, London Business School, and INSEAD.

Ms. Rogers has also served as a leader and member of project teams consulting on executive and leadership development strategies and implementation. Engagements where she has held leadership positions have included: creating and teaching a three year curriculum for the Deloitte US/India Leadership Academy, and executive programs for LG Group, Otsuka Pharmaceutical Company, Anritsu, Western Union, Digital Equipment Corporation, State Street Bank, Eisai Corporation, Bristol-Myers Squibb Corporation, the State of New York, and the Commonwealth of Massachusetts. She also works as an executive leadership coach with global clients.

Ms. Rogers is currently teaching in the Harvard Business online corporate executive education programs. She has served recently as the Faculty Co-Chair, Global Leaders Program, jointly sponsored by Berlitz with the Georgetown University McDonough School of Business, as well as in the adjunct faculty of the Nyenrode Business School, EMBA, Netherlands; University of New Hampshire, Whittemore School of Business; the University of Delaware, School of Business; the Villanova University, EMBA; the University of the West Indies, Mona Institute of Business; and the University of Budapest.

Ms. Rogers' approach in designing and facilitating learning is collaborative, coaching, conversational and collegial. Accessing the knowledge and insights of all creates a lively and engaging collective learning experience. In addition, she believes that leadership is from the 'inside out', and enables each leader to identify and harness their personal strengths, experiences and capabilities – their unique value.

Nick van Dam

Dr. Nick van Dam is a consultant, author, speaker, and researcher on corporate learning and leadership development. Keenly interested in how individuals learn and develop within organizations, his areas of expertise include setting organizational learning strategy, designing corporate academies, fostering leadership development, pursuing digital learning opportunities, managing learning and talent systems, inspiring social learning, improving performance management, driving change management, and boosting learning innovation.

As Global Chief Learning Officer at McKinsey, he is responsible for leading learning and leadership development for the Firm globally. In this role he provides thought leadership and operational oversight to drive the firm's broad-based learning agenda for continued innovation and impact. His primary areas of responsibility include shaping a learning agenda that is integrated with the Firm's strategic priorities, delivering world-class learning curricula for pivotal roles, ensuring the application of leading edge learning approaches including digital learning, operating a world class learning organization, and extending the Firm's external reach and relevance and client impact.

Before joining McKinsey, Nick was a senior executive for 19 years at Deloitte, where as the global chief learning officer, he shaped the learning and leadership development strategy and led a learning transformation. He also conducted research and was an advisor to more 100 clients globally.

Nick has authored and co-authored more than 15 books and numerous articles on change, organizational learning and leadership Development. He has been quoted by *The Financial Times, Fortune Magazine, Business Week, The India Times, Information Week, Management Consulting, CLO Magazine,* and *T+D Magazine.*

A visiting lecturer and advisory board member at the University of Pennsylvania, he works with candidates in the executive doctoral program for future chief learning officers. He is also a board member of ICEDR, an international consortium that promotes research and dialogue on global talent management, leadership development, and strategic change. He is Associate Professor at Nyenrode Business Universiteit.

Nick is the founder and chairman of *e-Learning for Kids*, a global non-profit foundation that offers digital lessons for underprivileged elementary-school aged children. Since 2005, more than 15 million children have benefitted from this free service.

In 2012, Nick received a Lifetime Learning Leadership Award from the MASIE Center, a think tank focused on workforce education and performance. The European Parliament Federal Ministry of Education & Research also granted him the Leonardo European Corporate Learning Award in 2013, in recognition of his efforts to direct the future of organizational learning and leadership development.

Made in the USA
Lexington, KY
11 May 2016